GHOST TOWNS
OF MANITOBA

GHOST TOWNS
OF MANITOBA

A RECORD OF PIONEER LIFE

Helen Mulligan & Wanda Ryder

GREAT PLAINS
PUBLICATIONS

Second Printing 2004

Great Plains Publications
420 – 70 Arthur Street
Winnipeg, MB R3B 1G7
www.greatplains.mb.ca

Great Plains Publications gratefully acknowledges the financial support provided for
its publishing program by the Government of Canada through the Book Publishing
Industry Development Program (BPIDP); the Canada Council for the Arts; as well
as the Manitoba Department of Culture, Heritage and Tourism; and the Manitoba
Arts Council.

Design & Typography by Gallant Design Ltd.
Printed in Canada by Friesens

CANADIAN CATALOGUING IN PUBLICATION DATA

Main entry under title:

Mulligan, Helen
  Ghost towns of Manitoba / Helen Mulligan, Wanda Ryder.

  ISBN 1-894283-41-4

  I. Ghost towns – Manitoba.   2. Manitoba – History, Local.   I. Ryder, Wanda.
II. Title.
FC3373.M86   2003   971.27'02   C2003-910810-4
F1063.M86   2003

DEDICATION

Cecil and Norma MacDonald
Elizabeth and Archbold Anderson,
Pioneers in their own time

CONTENTS

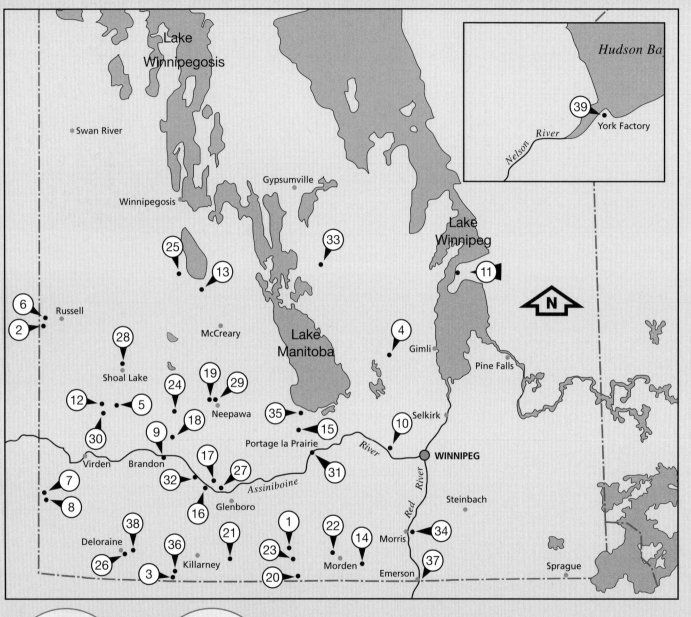

✳ LEGEND

Lake Winnipegosis

Hudson Bay

Swan River

York Factory

Nelson River

Gypsumville

Winnipegosis

Lake Winnipeg

25

33

13

11

N

6 Russell

2

28

McCreary

Lake Manitoba

4 Gimli

Pine Falls

19

24 29

12 5

30

18 Neepawa 35

9 15

10 Selkirk

Shoal Lake

17

WINNIPEG

Virden Brandon

32

27

31

7

Assiniboine

Steinbach

8

16 Glenboro

38

1 22

34

Deloraine

36 21 23 14 Morris

26

3 Killarney 20 Morden

37

Emerson

Sprague

Red River

River

✳ LEGEND

1   Archibald and Manitoba City
2   Asessippi
3   Bannerman
4   Bender Hamlet
5   Decker, Lavinia and McConnell
6   Dropmore
7   Ebor
8   Ewart
9   Grand Valley
10   Grantown
11   Hecla
12   Isabella
13   Makinak
14   Mennonite Villages
15   McArthur's Landing
16   Methven
17   Millford
18   Moore Park
19   Mountain Road
20   Mowbray
21   Neelin
22   Nelsonville
23   Norquay and Littleton
24   Odanah
25   Old Dauphin and Gartmore
26   Old Deloraine
27   Old Stockton, Stockton and Hilton
28   Olha, Seech and Horod
29   Polonia
30   Rea
31   Sioux Village
32   Souris City
33   Spearhill
34   Ste. Elizabeth
35   Totogan
36   Wakopa
37   West Lynne
38   Whitewater
39   York Factory

PREFACE

 URING OUR EXTENSIVE RESEARCH we visited well over 100 ghost town sites and travelled some 17,600 km or 11,000 miles. We found that the heaviest concentration of ghost towns was in the southcentral and southwest portion of the province.

Although we wanted equal representation from all areas, the trend of settlement and abandonment decided for us. The north was, and is, sparsely settled and the southeast corner offered few abandoned sites.

As well as trying to locate towns in all areas of the province, we tried for as much of an ethnic mix as possible in order to more fully convey the true character of the province. While many areas were settled by predominately British stock, there were also Aboriginal, Ukrainian, Polish, French, Jewish, Icelandic, Mennonite, Métis and others.

Once a ghost town had been identified and judged suitable for inclusion, came additional travelling to do research all over the province. Then there was the problem of photos. Many communities had so completely disappeared that the site was a field or pasture. We took many photos ourselves and sifted through thousands more at various archives. Individuals graciously loaned others.

During the years of research for the original book, published in 1985, and for the new, expanded and updated version, we received help from many people and organizations. People include Charlie Baldock; Bernice Blixhaven; Myrtle Burton; Pauline Chudzik; C.L. D'Aoust; Ina Dark; Jeanne Duprey; Donald Duprey; Aileen Garland; Frances Gillies; Les Henderson; Marion Koltusky; Marvin Krawec;

Dan Lewis; William Mason; Margaret Peech; Robert Radford; Yolande Rheault; Ida and Don Sanderson; Marsha Skrypuch; Roy Sitko; Sept Taylor; Lorette Vaughan; Dennis Wiens; Cindy Williams; and others in farmhouses and rural towns all over the province who supplied information and often a refreshing cup of tea as well.

With the passage of time since publication of the first book, some of the people named here or in the text are no longer living. We have tried to be sensitive to this reality in the updating and revision of the book.

Acknowledgement is also made with thanks to the Assiniboine Historical Society; Archibald Museum; Brandon Rural Resources; Daly House, Brandon; Historical and Scientific Society of Manitoba; Hudson's Bay Company Archives; Jewish Historical Society of Western Canada; Prairie Pens; Provincial Archives of Manitoba; Provincial Library of Manitoba; Portage la Prairie City Library; Public Archives of Canada; Surveys and Mapping Branch, Department of Energy, Mines and Resources; and the Royal Canadian Mounted Police.

Finally, the authors are grateful to family and friends, especially husbands Jim Mulligan and George Ryder for their continued support and encouragement.

— *Helen Mulligan and Wanda Ryder*

ARCHIBALD AND MANITOBA CITY

WOULD-BE SETTLERS TO THE PRAIRIES AS EARLY AS THE 1870s were bombarded with contradictory reports from promoters and governments. Glowing advertisements in Ontario papers wooed with promises such as: "You can easily own one of the best farms in the West. All it requires is a small amount of capital, pluck and energy." But not all accounts were so glowing. An English journal, for instance, noted: "The Canadian Pacific Railway, if it is ever finished, will run through a country about as forbidding as any on earth…In Manitoba those who are not frozen to death are often maimed for life by frostbites."

The courageous and enterprising ignored such predictions of disaster and came anyway. Among them was Alex Bethune who arrived in 1878. He established a homestead at the junction of the Old Hunter's Trail and the Brandon House Trail near present-day Manitou. Then he opened a store and post office which he named Archibald. Bethune's brother, John, settled nearby but didn't long remain a homesteader. It was an era when speculation prevailed as settlers anticipated burgeoning towns and cities sure to come in the wake of the railways. When John Bethune was offered $5,600 for his holdings by John Stewart, a railway contractor, he quickly accepted since the property had cost only a $10 homestead fee.

But Bethune didn't just take the money and leave. He and his brother, Alex, shrewdly reasoning that Stewart wouldn't have purchased the land unless he knew that the railway was going to run through it, made plans to share in the upcoming bonanza. On ten acres surrounding the buildings on Alex's property at the junction of the two pioneer trails, they laid out a townsite they called Archibald.

They also had a contingency plan in case the railway passed to the west. Land was available in the area they selected but cash was scarce. To solve the problem Alex Bethune formed a partnership with a friend who was also an agent in the National Investment Company. They bought the land and optimistically surveyed still another townsite.

In the meantime, the extra-curricular activities of some railway officials had aroused suspicion in the CPR's top echelon. They sent Cornelius Van Horne to investigate. He soon discovered that there was indeed a problem. Railway contractor John Stewart – the man

Opposite: One of the earliest "roads" in southern Manitoba was the Boundary Commission Trail, shown crossing the Souris River in the early 1870s. Most pioneers, however, didn't have even the luxury of a trail and had to build their own.

who had bought John Bethune's property – had been told the location of the terminus of the railway's Pembina Mountain branch line by general manager Alpheus Stickney. Although Stickney was fired and the branch route changed, Stewart was not greatly concerned. He already owned land at the proposed terminus 3.2 km (2 miles) south of Archibald townsite.

The fate of the Bethune townsites was revealed when the CPR announced a route change and explained the reason in a report carried by the *Manitoba Free Press* on January 23, 1882: "By keeping closer to Darlingford all of the bad curvatures are avoided. The road terminates…two miles from Archibald and exactly 100 miles from Winnipeg. About 80 miles of this has already been graded and the balance will be completed early in the spring, when track laying will commence, and the whole line will be finished by November the 1st next…

"The public will see by the above authoritative announcement that the terminus of this important railway has been finally and definitely located on the Townsite of Manitoba City. The new town is situated on a beautiful spot of rolling prairie near the Pembina River Valley. It will be the business centre of that large block of well settled townships known as the Pembina Mountain District – the choicest part of south-western Manitoba."

The report goes on to say that lots in Manitoba City were "…offered for sale in blocks and numerous sales have already been made at handsome prices for cash and without advertisement." It ends with the information that; "The purchase was made from John Stewart, contractor for a section on the line, who retains an interest in the site."

Since Manitoba City was heralded not only as a terminus but "quite possibly" a junction of many other railways, lots became a popular investment. The railway, too, proceeded quickly in spite of spring flooding in the Red River Valley. On December 1, 1882, it reported that twice a week "a train will run from the Pembina Junction, through the fertile regions of south-western Manitoba to Manitoba City." Eleven days later, the name of Manitoba City appeared for the first time on the CPR time-table.

The bright hopes of John Stewart seemed justified when the railway arrived almost on schedule. True, the lateness of the year had caused work to stop before a turnaround "Y" had been built, obliging train crews to back up 72 km (45 miles) over mostly unballasted track. Also, the rails didn't quite reach the new townsite and freight was dumped into a ditch, causing breakage, loss and frayed tempers. Passengers were deposited in the same unceremonious fashion.

MANITOBA CITY'S FIRST GROCERY STORE WAS ORIGINALLY HOUSED IN A TENT ON CITY MARKET SQUARE BUT WAS SOON REPLACED BY A FRAME BUILDING.

Still, with the railway close enough that residents could hear the whistle on a calm night, building commenced at a rate that kept three lumber yards supplying materials. Other business places that started included three grain buyers, with one of the lumber dealers even branching into grain buying. Another started a cattle business and became the largest buyer of cattle and hogs in Manitoba. Huge cattle drives with dozens of cowboys left Manitoba City to cross the plains some 1,400 km (900 miles) to Alberta.

Manitoba City's first grocery store was originally housed in a tent on City Market Square but was soon replaced by a frame building. Not to be left behind, Alex Bethune moved all there ever was of Archibald – the store and post office – to Stewart's new town. It became Manitoba City's second business. Other general stores opened, as well as three hardware stores, harness shop, butcher shop and a large, diversified drug store with a jewellery department. There were even a carriage maker,

Manitoba City _Dec 16 1884_

Mr Stollinger

Bot. of Francis & Fowler,
IMPORTERS OF
DRY GOODS, GROCERIES, BOOTS, SHOES, &c., &c

Sold by   Exd. by

To Turkey 32 lbs
C /ct   4.00
" 74 lbs chicken   7.40
11.40

undertaker, five livery stables and nine farm implement agencies.

Because the community was at the end of steel, it served at least a dozen settlements, including Snowflake, Crystal City, Pilot Mound and Glenboro. To cater to the increasing number of businessmen and other travellers, John Stewart's brother built the first hotel. It was soon followed by five others, all licensed to sell liquor. Since there were two wholesale liquor outlets as well, residents didn't lack places to purchase the ingredients to ward off the evening chill. A spin-off from these liquor outlets was increased employment. Twelve Justices of the Peace were appointed to prevent the boom town from roaring too loudly.

Residents of the budding metropolis were busy and optimistic – so optimistic that they paid little attention to surveying activity just south of their town. Those who did notice probably assumed it was a planned extension of Manitoba City. This assumption was to have traumatic consequences, especially for businessmen. The surveying was for an extension – but not to Manitoba City.

The perpetrators were lawyers with CPR connections. Two of them, William Ellis and Corbette Locke, had earlier acquired the same information as John Stewart – the location of the railway's terminus. Not to be outdone by Stewart, and hoping to share in the land boom, they had bought two quarter sections adjoining the existing townsite a week before Stewart's Manitoba City lots went on sale.

Stewart grudgingly welcomed the newcomers and told them they could register their land as part of Manitoba City. With this promise, they began surveying and aligned their streets with his. The crafty Stewart waited until the survey was completed then withdrew his offer, disallowing them any association with Manitoba City, including the use of the name.

Ellis and Locke were disappointed and Locke sold his interests to another lawyer, H.A. Jukes, who was also a surveyor with the CPR engineering department. When the CPR started marking the grade for the much needed "Y" in the spring of 1883, Jukes was in charge. Stewart now paid for his unethical treatment of the rival townsite promoters. For reasons not difficult to understand, Jukes ran the survey across the townsite belonging to himself and Ellis, completely by-passing Stewart's townsite.

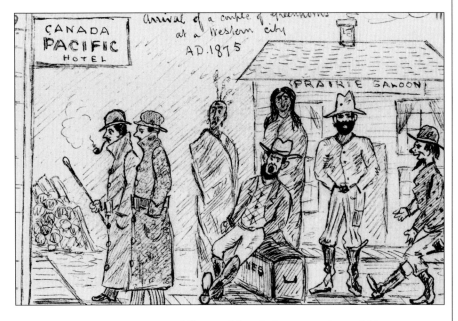

Above: Get rich schemes abounded in Manitoba City – and in other prairie towns of the time. Greenhorns hoping for a piece of the pie quite often earned only derision, as in this 1875 sketch.

After restaking their town so it would have no connection with Manitoba City, the lawyers offered the CPR a generous amount of land for the right to have the station in their town. Then they arranged with Ogilvie Milling Company to erect an elevator at the end of the line.

By late summer there was no doubt that the skillfully executed double-cross had doomed Manitoba City.

On September 29 Nelsonville's *Manitoba Mountaineer* understated the fact: "It is said that a rival town is laid out on the south side of the tracks at Manitoba City." In October, apparently still not entirely convinced, the paper reported: "There is a rumour afloat that the name of Manitoba City is to be changed to Manitou."

Indeed, the Aboriginal name of Manitou, meaning "great spirit," had been chosen that summer by the CPR's Land Commissioner. That December Manitou replaced Manitoba City on the railway's time-table and the migration began.

The first business to move down the hill to the new townsite was Fullerton and Ross's General Store – the one which had started in a tent. Most of the other businesses followed, including five hotels. Even Stewart House, a large three-storey building, made the trip without incident.

Whether it regarded Manitoba City as a bad joke or as an embarrassment is not clear, but the local paper, the *Manitoba Mercury*, never referred to it by name. Instead, in reference to a relocation it noted: "The Pioneer Store, and we might add, its good-natured proprietor, has grown in size and importance since moving over from the old site at Archibald."

Manitoba City was the victim of the plots and counter-plots common in the days of settlement and rail building. Bethune, the man who started it all, kept up with the migrations. In 1884, shortly after moving his store and post office from Archibald to Manitoba City, he trundled it to Manitou where he ran it for several years before selling and moving to other highly successful ventures. For some reason the post office was called Archibald for five years before finally being changed to Manitou.

Perhaps postal authorities were waiting to see if the new community was less nomadic than its predecessors. It was – and is today a pleasant community of nearly 1300 people.

ASESSIPPI

 SESSIPPI, PROBABLY THE MOST BEAUTIFUL ghost town site in Manitoba, is located on the banks of the Shell River just northwest of Inglis on Highway 3. The vanished village was named by combining two Cree words, "asess" meaning "shell," and "sippi" meaning "river."

The earliest known reference to the area was made in 1794 by John Sutherland of the Hudson's Bay Company. He wrote in his journal: "Got to the Shell River where there are settlements, one for ye N.W. Co. (North West Company) and another for Peter Grant. I think of stopping here as ye season is too far advanced to proceed further this year." The next year he stated in a letter: "I am a person in charge at a place called Essa Seepy by the natives, or Shell River."

It was almost 100 years later before permanent settlers arrived. In 1882, a group of men were granted a charter by the Dominion government to form the Shell River Colonization Company. Its purpose was to encourage further settlement in the district and to make a profit from the influx of settlers. Henry Gill was sent to act as overseer. His tenure was short-lived, though, as the venture failed. The Shell River Colonization Company was dissolved but Gill, who envisioned other business opportunities, stayed at Asessippi.

When he learned that the first postmaster had died he purchased the building which housed the post office and moved it into the Shell River Valley. Here he re-opened with himself as postmaster. Then, with his two sons and Fred Richardson Sr., he built a store which soon flourished. An 1893 advertisement in the *Russell Chronicle and Free Advertiser* noted: "J.A. Gill, General Merchant. Complete stock of goods always on hand at lowest prices. Highest prices paid for furs. We are always up to the times. Asessippi."

According to the memoirs written by pioneer resident Mrs. Amice Robin, "...the store would be open late every night and the men would gather around the big box stove and swap stories of the 'Good Old Days' when there were herds of buffalo on the west plains to hunt, and the way they would spot herds from the hill tops and how they would stalk them."

As well as doing a brisk business in merchandise, the store provided other facilities. Mrs. Robin noted that the store was "…a large building in those days with an outside stair leading to the second storey. This room was used for entertainments, church and weddings." In addition, the back of the store served as a boarding house for several years.

Successful in the store venture, the Gill family, Richardson and two other men formed the Asessippi Milling Company and began building a dam just above the bridge over the Shell River. The mills they built were described in 1889 in a booklet compiled by G.G. Meikie, editor and publisher of *The Canadian Siftings:* "About twelve miles north of Russell is situated the village Asessippi on the Shell River. The water-power of this river has been utilized, and a Roller Process Flour Mill constructed in 1883 is now running and there is also a Lumber and Shingle Mill all run by turbines."

Because it was the only flour mill for miles, it enjoyed good patronage and also provided employment for many local men. In addition, the mill furnished customers for the boarding house since farmers bringing their grain from long distances had to stay overnight.

The sawmill also prospered. At first, nearby timber was used but later logs from the Duck Mountains were floated down the river in a huge spring log drive. Buoyed by the success of their combined milling operations and the promise of the Manitoba and North Western Railway to build through the Shell Valley, the owners started a brick yard.

With the future seemingly assured, others were encouraged to go into business. A cheese factory was built to provide a market for surplus milk, and a blacksmith shop and feed barn appeared in the early 1890s, as did a church and a school. While the Gills provided much of the energy and initiative, others contributed to the business and social life of the community. Jim Munro, who was in charge of the brick kiln, was not only a skilled brick maker but also a hunter, trapper, lumberjack, hunting-dog trainer and an excellent marksman.

Another who contributed to the life of the town was school teacher Charles Wright. His enthusiasm ranged from giving music lessons on an organ he had brought with him to helping children build sleds. With the sleds the youngsters were able to make the surrounding hills a delightful winter playground and their musical training ensured a continuing supply of church organists following Wright's departure.

One group who furnished entertainment were the Remittance Men. These men, usually well educated, were sent from England by their families (for reasons best known to themselves) and were funded by them. The object − not always attained − was to have these inexperienced men live with Canadian farm families to learn agricultural skills.

As Mrs. Robin noted: "…having lots of money they could spend most of their time hunting amusements. In the summer on the west plains they had horse racing, drawing crowds from all the outside districts. Then, in winter, the older men organized a curling rink, naming it the Shell-Asessippi Curling Club. Their games were curled on the river below Gill's home and there was a curling match whenever enough men gathered together."

The first "rocks" used for these games were improvised by cutting blocks of wood from black poplar trees. The blocks were cut at the sawmill a year or so before they were to be used, allowing them to dry slowly to prevent cracking. Then they were buried in oat bins and removed periodically to be coated with linseed oil. When the blocks were properly seasoned, they were fitted with iron handles. Until 1889, when the club purchased granite curling stones, these home-made rocks substituted admirably.

THE OBJECT − NOT ALWAYS ATTAINED − WAS TO HAVE THESE INEXPERIENCED MEN LIVE WITH CANADIAN FARM FAMILIES TO LEARN AGRICULTURAL SKILLS.

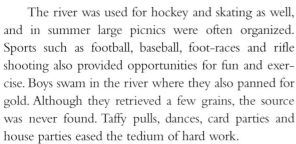

The river was used for hockey and skating as well, and in summer large picnics were often organized. Sports such as football, baseball, foot-races and rifle shooting also provided opportunities for fun and exercise. Boys swam in the river where they also panned for gold. Although they retrieved a few grains, the source was never found. Taffy pulls, dances, card parties and house parties eased the tedium of hard work.

Unfortunately, Asessippi's good times came to an end rather abruptly – even for those uncertain days. The mills – the economic basis of the community – were beset by problems. Partly because of poor engineering, the mill dam and the bridge were washed out by ice and water three times. In spite of the company's costly repairs to the dam and bridge, the lumber mill failed because of poor demand for its products.

The flour mill continued for a time since its reputation for high quality baking flour and cream of wheat was excellent. It finally closed because of competition from the larger milling companies in Russell. The cheese factory also proved unsuccessful. Farmers found travelling up to 64 km (40 miles) by horse and wagon to deliver milk difficult and uneconomical.

While loss of these industries darkened the future, worse was to come. In 1896 the Manitoba and North Western Railway reneged on its promise to continue through the Shell Valley and stopped 19 km (12 miles) south at Russell. Then in 1902 the few remaining residents had their last hopes shattered. They believed that another railway, the Canadian Northern, would build into their community. But it chose a route 32 km (20 miles) north. The brick kiln closed, the blacksmith packed up his horseshoes, anvil and other equipment and moved to nearby Foxwarren. Gill sold his store and residents began the sad exodus from their beloved valley.

Today, ruins of the bridge and several dilapidated buildings on both sides of the river are the only direct links to the past. Nevertheless, the energy and enterprise still evident in towns and farms in the Asessippi area is a reminder that the spirit of those first settlers lives on.

Left: c. 1980. remnant of Asessippi's past.

Above: Overlooking what was once Asessippi, probably "…the most beautiful ghost town site in Manitoba."

BANNERMAN

BANNERMAN WAS UNIQUE IN THAT DURING ITS HEYDAY there wasn't a decent road to the community – even by 1900 standards. Access was by wagon tracks and trails that meandered across country, through the bush and over the International Border four km (2 1/2 miles) away. The easiest way to reach Bannerman was by travelling to Desford, or St. John, in North Dakota and riding the train. Ironically, although there is today a graded road, there is no community for it to serve. Nor is an orange-painted boulder inscribed "Bannerman Population 3" still relevant. It was painted in 1967 by Bannerman's last residents of the time, the Les Henderson family. They moved out in 1980 and now only cellar depressions, a house, and a patch of garden flowers gone wild suggest that a town once flourished here.

Bannerman was given life by the old Brandon, Saskatchewan and Hudson Bay Railway which railway magnate Jim Hill connected with his Great Northern at St. John and dreamed of pushing all the way to Hudson Bay. "It never got much past Brandon, though," said Alvie Spafford, an early Bannerman resident interviewed in a Brandon nursing home during the 1980s.

Spafford, a witness to the coming of the railroad and the growth of the town, recalled how there was nothing at Bannerman but prairie until the BS & HS came through in 1905. "Then a man by the name of Jack Downs bought the townsite and sold lots," he said. "He had a sawmill back in the Turtle Mountains in North Dakota and he sawed out poplar and sold the lumber to build the houses. He had a good thing going; he made

some money and we never saw him again. He started a good little town though."

Bannerman was the Canadian port of entry on the BS & HB railway (locally referred to as the Great Northern). Its customs house and quarantine barn became the nucleus of a thriving business community that supported a population of 250 in its peak years. Business places included several stores, livery barn, harness shop, the usual combination of poolroom and barbershop, and a dance hall. There was also a puffed wheat factory, an elevator, railway station, jail, hotel and a church where, according to a former townsman, "Anyone that came along could preach if he liked."

Old-timers exchanged tales about the "rather impressive" ten-room hotel where "You stood up against

Opposite: The Great Northern that served Bannerman from 1905 to 1936. It was also known as "Charlie's Train" after Charlie Bryant, conductor for over thirty years.

the bar and ordered your whiskey by the glass or in a bottle if you wanted." They talked about the mild-mannered proprietor who "didn't know much about money" but just kept pouring as the dozen or so jokesters at the bar took turns pushing forward the same 25 cent-piece with the request to "fill 'em up, Pete."

They spoke of the barroom brawl that almost ended in murder when a man pulled the trigger on a gun that didn't fire, even though there was an indentation on the cartridge where the firing pin hit. They related how, when the United States "went dry" in 1920, whiskey was hauled out of Bannerman in democrats, wagons, and sleighs, and that one hotel owner retired from inn-keeping and began rum running as an occupation. He had an old car, which he drove at ten miles an hour and though no one thought he was doing anything unusual, he was operating a profitable bootlegging business.

The nearby bush-land with its network of trails provided cover for this illicit activity and a safe, if circuitous, route to the border. It also provided shelter for a number of bush-dwellers described by one area farmer as "real losers."

"They didn't want to get ahead themselves and they didn't want anyone else to," he said. "If they thought you were getting ahead they soon did something to bring you down. Even the kids. If a kid showed up at school with his lunch in a new jam pail they took it and kicked it around until it looked like theirs. They'd drag a kid through the mud if he looked clean."

But there were good neighbours, too. Possibly the best remembered among them was Charlie Bryant, conductor for more than thirty years on the BS & HB passenger train. "Charlie's Train," as it became known, ran daily (except Sunday) between Brandon, Manitoba, and St. John, North Dakota. Conductor Bryant, who was also a farmer, sometimes sorted his seed grain as he travelled but he was never too busy to assist a fellow-farmer or extend an extra courtesy to passengers.

…WHEN THE UNITED STATES "WENT DRY" IN 1920, WHISKEY WAS HAULED OUT OF BANNERMAN IN DEMOCRATS, WAGONS, AND SLEIGHS…

Alvie Spafford recalled his kindness during a winter storm when Spafford's ailing son had to be transported by train to hospital in Brandon: "Charlie Bryant kept the train waiting for us at Boissevain while a doctor treated my boy. He said, 'Take all the time you need; when you say you're done then we'll go on'."

Others remembered the times that Bryant stopped the train between stations to accommodate harvest workers and berry pickers. And they spoke of the 'midway' train, when elephants and horses were let out to graze at Bannerman and how it seemed "like the Brandon Fair right there at the station." There were memories of the special excursion trains to Brandon, and the train crews going for supper at the Bannerman Hotel where they could get anything on the menu for 25 cents.

It was an era of "great good times" for the railroaders and their patrons but it would not last. The depression of the 1930s brought a reduction in freight business and passenger traffic. Then, when the company's thirty-year mail contract expired and was not renewed, the train service ended. Tracks were torn up and by 1937 the pioneer railway was only a memory.

Business places closed and townspeople moved away. In the vacated railway station a store and post office lingered for another twenty years but now they, too, are gone.

Below: Bannerman in its early years.

BENDER HAMLET

ENDER HAMLET, IN THE INTERLAKE COUNTRY BETWEEN LAKE MANITOBA and Lake Winnipeg, was the site of the first Jewish farm colony in Manitoba. In 1902, when Jacob Bender bought the property and travelled to England and Russia to encourage Jewish immigration to his new town, it seemed to these oppressed people that he offered a bright new "promised land."

Hounded from the villages of Czarist Russia, the Jews had been restricted to living within the Pale of Settlement since 1791. (When Russia expropriated parts of Poland the Polish Jews were confined to a particular area which came to be called the "Pale, or Boundary, of Settlement.") They needed permission to live in the cities, many of their children were denied schooling and, beginning in 1827, their boys could be conscripted into the Russian army for twenty-five years. Many left the country during the next several years in a migration reminiscent of the ancient Jewish exodus from Egypt. The unfortunate thousands who remained in Russia, however, faced increasing persecution.

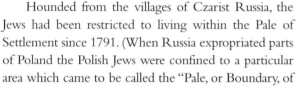

In his book, *Through Narrow Gates*, Simon Belkin reports an estimated $80 million property damage and over 100,000 Jews rendered homeless in government-organized pogroms in the early 1880s. In 1891 another 200,000 Jews were dispossessed. As the refugees fled across the Russian border various committees were formed in other countries to assist them.

In Canada a colonization committee formed in 1890 by the Young Men's Hebrew Benevolent Society got its start on funds received from Jewish philanthropist Baron Maurice de Hirsch. The committee's primary aim was farm colonization in western Canada where they envisioned a settlement "of 5,000 to 10,000 Jews...in Manitoba or in the North-West Territories." By the turn of the century three small settlements had started west of the Manitoba border, although one of them had already collapsed due to recurrent crop failures and a disastrous fire.

The Russian Jews who accepted Bender's proposal for farming in the Interlake were dazzled by expectations of freedom, prosperity, and the means to rescue rel-

Opposite: Winter frosts heaved up annual crops of rocks in the fields.

Centre: Immigrants arriving at Bender Colony in the early 1900s.

atives from the old country. Not even the prospect of an arduous sea-voyage and the 3,000 km (1,800 mile) journey across a new continent daunted them. The hazards of the journey, however, were all too real.

A.J. Arnold in *The Beaver* magazine writes of a Jewish family of the period who travelled from the Ukraine with four children. The eldest was entrusted with a copper kettle filled with gooseberry preserves intended to combat sea-sickness. But the six-week journey caused such illness that the entire family was unable even to taste the preserves and the kettle of fruit arrived in Winnipeg untouched.

Another settler wrote after his arrival: "Every one of our bodies are bruised from top to bottom. Our hearts still shaken from the terror of the cross (sic) of the sea."

To add to their misery the settlers discovered that much of the land at Bender Hamlet was stony and hard. The soil either would not retain water or was too wet, and the stands of coveted timber proved difficult to market as there was no railway to the area, which lay 80 km (50 miles) north of Winnipeg. They nevertheless settled into their new existence with thankfulness, freedom itself being a powerful incentive.

Bender's townsite was divided into nineteen lots, including one for the "shul" (synagogue). They were strung along one side of the road in the European "Strassendorf" style. Upon payment of a small government registration fee each family received a quarter section of land close to the village.

Eighteen families, including two from Winnipeg and one from Boston, arrived in the summer of 1902 and began to build their homes. As there was not enough time before winter to complete homes for everyone, several families lived together until spring.

The houses were set on concrete foundations with basements built of limestone gathered from the fields. The walls of squared spruce logs were chinked with a mixture of clay, manure and straw. "We mixed it with our feet," one pioneer noted. "Later on when they could afford it they had horses to do the mixing – but not at the beginning."

The log homes, little more than 5m x 7m (16' x 23'), were sturdily built, shingled with cedar and whitewashed inside and out. A gingerbread trim completed the exterior. Inside, furnishings were simple and sparse. But each family would affix to the doorjambs a "mezuzah," a small case containing a piece of parchment inscribed with verses from the Torah, reminding them that they were God's chosen people. As well, there

Above: Settlers chinked their log homes with a mixture of clay, manure and straw.

Below: Bender Hamlet in 1920.

would be ceremonial religious objects such as the Kiddush cup, Hadas (spicebox) and the Chanuka candelabra, or a lamp.

Like their people the world over, the Orthodox Jews of Bender Hamlet observed the various religious festivals and traditions of their forefathers. On Fridays at sundown, as the Sabbath was about to begin, the mother of the family would light two candles on the supper table. As she did so she recited the traditional blessing: "Blessed art Thou, O Lord, our God, King of the Universe, who has sanctified us in His commandments and commanded us to light the Sabbath light."

After the "Kiddush" (a prayer of sanctification) was offered by the father, he sipped from a wine cup then passed it to his wife and perhaps the children. No matter how poor the family, a blessing was said over two Sabbath loaves meant to indicate that the Sabbath meal is especially abundant. In fact, though, sometimes the loaves were simple bannock made with bitter flour milled from frozen wheat and the Kiddush wine obtained from a few fermented raisins.

But, poor or not, life in the Hamlet was never tragic or dull. Writer Ted Allan notes in the *Winnipeg Free Press* that the village "...exuded vitality and thrived on optimism." The settlers enjoyed "parties and picnics, games and fairs, bar mitzvahs and weddings, the holidays and festivals. There was shul (synagogue) every Saturday, Hebrew lessons for the children in the evening after conventional school...The children were robust, exuberant, prankish. The adults were free to exist communally, to co-exist, or to compete with one another."

Their greatest competition, however, came from the land itself and the harsh climate of the Canadian prairie. Early frosts and hail killed the crops, while dairy cattle strayed and lived half-wild in the bush for weeks at a time. Worse, each winter's frosts heaved up a new harvest of rocks in the fields.

In spite of the hardships the life of the settlers gradually improved and the Hamlet grew to a peak in 1915 of about 130 people. It had one or more general stores, a livery, feed and sales stable, and a boarding house, which became a haven for travellers in the sparsely populated region. The community even had its own "shochet," a Jewish slaughterer authorized to perform ritual slaughter in accordance with dietary laws.

Markets for beef, cordwood and lumber, grain and dairy products opened in 1914 when the Canadian Northern Railway built a line 4 km (2 1/2 miles) west of the Hamlet. The station was named Narcisse in honour of a president of the Jewish Colonization Association. Encouraged by the new railway, the settlers built a creamery and cheese factory nearby. One raised horses that were shipped as far away as Montreal while another expanded his dairy herd to 600.

But prosperity came too late to Bender Hamlet. Cattle prices fell after World War One and three successive crop failures beginning in 1924 struck the village a mortal blow. Its demise, though, had begun as early as 1915 when several of the original settlers gave up the struggle and departed for Winnipeg and other towns. They were replaced for a while by new immigrants but the trend, once started, did not cease.

A strong factor in the failure of the colony, according to Bender Hamlet native Jack Lavitt, was its Orthodox religion. He is quoted by Ted Allan in the *Winnipeg Free Press:* "…In those years our people

"…IN THOSE YEARS OUR PEOPLE DIDN'T WANT TO INTERMARRY…THERE WEREN'T ENOUGH YOUNG PEOPLE TO GO AROUND. SO, THEY STARTED LEAVING."

didn't want to intermarry…There weren't enough young people to go around. So, they started leaving." Once the young people were gone there was no one to carry on the work. People would sell everything by auction, Lavitt recalled: "Furniture, chickens, livestock, machinery, outbuildings. Then they'd just walk away and let the land revert to the crown."

Writing of the abandonment in *Jewish Life in Canada*, William Kurelek had this to say: "Those who stuck it out the longest left the area with many memories, both happy and sad ones…These memories are like the voices in the wind as it sighs through the thistles of the overgrown fields and through the chinks of abandoned buildings."

But now even the old buildings are gone. All that remains are basement depressions and a few half-hidden graves in the brush.

Below: Hauling water by oxcart in 1925.

DECKER, LAVINIA AND McCONNELL

"THESE ARE A LOVELESS BUNCH. They don't love each other as there hasn't been a wedding. The Lord doesn't love them for he hasn't called anyone away. Finally, they don't love me for they didn't give me all my salary."

With these words a young student minister summed up the early 1900s social and economic life in the communities of Decker, Lavinia and McConnell. He had to travel by rail 418 km (260 miles) from Winnipeg to Hamiota (the nearest station) and then make his way on horseback 30 km (19 miles) to serve these small communities. But his problems were minor compared with those encountered by the pioneers who preceded him to the area in the early 1880s.

The settlements, located 161 km (100 miles) northwest of Brandon, were accessible only in summer when sternwheel steamers plied the Assiniboine River to Fort Ellice. From various landings along the way, settlers disembarked and continued their journeys over prairie trails travelling by Red River cart or horse and buggy. Not until the arrival of the Canadian Northern Railway a quarter of a century later was their transportation problem eased.

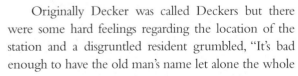

In 1910, the villages of Decker, Lavinia and McConnell were founded. Their names stem from the fact that different systems were used for naming the scores of towns, villages and stations during the early settlement of Manitoba. The Canadian Pacific Railway tended to name new settlements after their employees. The Grand Trunk Railway used alphabetical order such as Oakner, Pope, Quadra and Rea while the Canadian Northern favoured the use of settlers' names. Thus Decker was named for A.L. Decker, a member of the Canadian Northern's survey gang, since the station was on his land. Lavinia and McConnell honoured pioneer residents Lavinia Hoy and A.D. McConnell.

Originally Decker was called Deckers but there were some hard feelings regarding the location of the station and a disgruntled resident grumbled, "It's bad enough to have the old man's name let alone the whole

Left: A vacant store at Decker. Communities could survive drought and other natural disasters but not the loss of the railway.

family!" The "s" was thereafter dropped. The Decker family nevertheless remained a vital force in the new community and their home was always open to travellers.

Growth was steady in the new villages. Ernie Youngson, who grew up in Decker, described the village of his youth: "We had trains on Monday, Wednesday and Friday evenings. Friday was the big night because all the district farmers came in, along with their families. Supplies were bought for the week, deals were made and it was regarded as a general get-together. We boys would chase the farmers' daughters. It was fun night!"

For other kinds of fun, debating societies were formed and dancing was very popular. Enthusiastic dancers often came the eight km (five miles) to Decker from Lavinia, danced all night and returned home on the morning train. It may even be that "streaking" was born in this district when a young man, miffed because he had not been invited to a wedding, put in a memorable but brief appearance – in the nude!

Residents, however, usually confined themselves to more conserva-tive pastimes such as skating and curling. The Norton farm, just north of Decker, had a race track and this attractively landscaped farm was also used for community sports days and picnics.

When Ernie Youngson left the district in 1940, he recalled that Decker still had the following services: "A railway station, two elevators, stock yards, livery stable, black-smith, Beaver Lumber, a garage, a Ford dealer, B.A. gasoline station, two stores, a Memorial Hall, United Church, Apostolic Mission, post office, and a big four-room school. Also a railway section gang, curling and skating rinks and a town dray."

The nearby villages of Lavinia and McConnell were about the same size as Decker. None, however, was able to survive the competition provided by good highways to larger centres and the loss of the railway in the 1970s. Decker dwindled to a few families and post office, transfer company, bulk oil station and the Birdtail River School Division bus terminal.

IT MAY EVEN BE THAT "STREAKING" WAS BORN IN THIS DISTRICT WHEN A YOUNG MAN, MIFFED BECAUSE HE HAD NOT BEEN INVITED TO A WEDDING, PUT IN A MEMORABLE BUT BRIEF APPEARANCE – IN THE NUDE!

By the early 1980s there were still several families and a garage at Lavinia, but in McConnell, nine km (six miles) east, only one family remained and there were no businesses left. Although all three pioneer settlements were surrounded by thriving and prosperous farms, they are now little more than names on a map and memories in the minds of a few old-timers.

Centre: Mr. And Mrs. Bill Thompson, in 1980 the last residents of McConnell.

Below: The railway station at McConnell after the tracks were lifted.

DROPMORE

ROPMORE, RENOWNED AS THE HOME OF PIONEER HORTICULTURIST plant breeder Frank Leith Skinner, got its name in an unusual way. An early resident recalls that when the railway was completed in 1909 many of the district men gathered in the caboose of the last work train to celebrate the event. When it was agreed that they should have "one drop more" in honour of the occasion, it led to the naming of the station – Dropmore.

As with most other prairie towns, it was rumours of a proposed railway that brought the first settlers in 1883. They took up homesteads, mostly on the west side of the Assiniboine River since it was less heavily wooded and abundance of pasture and water made it suitable for ranching. When it became clear three years later that they had been bypassed by the Manitoba and North Western Railway many settlers moved out. The tenacious few who stayed weathered a disastrous drought which lasted from 1889 until 1892, resulting in a critical feed shortage. Desperate ranchers saved some cattle by painstakingly shovelling snow from the ground to expose grass for the starving animals.

During this difficult time, men started gold mining in the Shell River. With their rockers and sluice boxes they worked the almost-dry riverbed, some old-timers boasting of finding $2 - $3 worth a day. While this return was excellent pay, most did not prosper.

The future brightened considerably in the early 1900s when new rumours of a railway brought another rush of homesteaders. Then sawmills were established on the western edge of the Riding Mountains and more people arrived. Fortunately, the railway rumours were correct this time and in 1909 the Canadian Northern Railway arrived at Dropmore.

With the railway came an elevator built by the British North America Company and a bridge over the Shell River. These developments encouraged more grain growing in the area since it was no longer necessary to make the long 48 km (28 mile) haul to Roblin or 35 km (22 miles) to Russell. A branch of the Grain Growers Association was formed and later another elevator was built by the United Grain Growers. Two stores, a post office and a cement block factory were among business places opened.

The first school appeared in 1911 but it would be over forty years before a church was constructed. For years church service was conducted in private homes and, later, in a log church in Castleavery, approximately 14 km (9 miles) southwest. The church itself was a

THE TENACIOUS FEW WHO STAYED WEATHERED A DISASTROUS DROUGHT WHICH LASTED FROM 1889 UNTIL 1892, RESULTING IN A CRITICAL FEED SHORTAGE.

Right: Although Dropmore has virtually disappeared, its place in history is assured by famous and self-taught horticulturist, the late Frank Leith Skinner.

Above: An old store in the almost deserted village.

memorial, paid for with money donated by Mrs. Fullerton of England whose son was one of three men killed in the district when a boiler exploded during harvest. The memorial church was later burned in a prairie fire and services moved to a school until Dropmore Community Hall was built.

During Dropmore's formative years, a district resident was quietly following his intense interest in horticulture. He was Frank Leith Skinner who had come from England with his parents in 1895 when he was thirteen. His skills in plant breeding were to make the village famous and be a major contribution to his adopted country.

In his book, *Horticultural Horizons*, Dr. Skinner described the Dropmore area in 1895 as being one of the outposts of farming communities: "To give an idea of the sparsity of farming settlement at the time, one

threshing outfit run by the power of ten horses threshed all the grain grown north of Asessippi and between the Riding Mountains and the Saskatchewan border." (This was an area covering over 200 square miles.)

Since the only real cash crop was beef cattle, the Skinner family began ranching. Although a lung problem in 1901 restricted Frank's ranching activities, it gave him time to study and to correspond with others of comparable interests. He was particularly interested in plants from countries which had climates similar to that of the prairies. During this time he also began a garden which was eventually to become internationally known as Skinner's Nursery.

The long hours spent on horseback tending cattle now proved invaluable for he had developed skills of observation and noted various plant associations among the native vegetation. Also, his perceptive interest taught him much about the laws of heredity. He said of the time: "A quick ride through the herd would usually be sufficient to tell me if some of them had strayed away, if they had, a ride around the ground where the herd had fed lately would probably show the direction taken by the strays and a faded leaf or two would give a clue as to the time since the animals had passed that way.

"All this may seem to the scientific plant breeder or to the professional collector to have little bearing on the problems of plant breeding. But to one who did not have the advantage of university training it was a very valuable experience."

Skinner realized that when the settlers finally had time to grow shrubs and trees for ornamental purposes they would find their choices very restricted. Plants from their milder homelands weren't sufficiently hardy nor were those from eastern and western North America. "I began to collect plants in 1911," Skinner wrote, "and to introduce plants from other countries in 1918. While much material was obtained on collection trips, much more was obtained through correspondence with individuals and institutes in various countries."

Developing specimens that would prove hardy in the harsh prairie climate was Skinner's primary concern and it demanded long, tedious work. He was quoted in *The Russell Banner*, February 4, 1965: "To lay out plans of what you intend to get, and what you do get, can be two different things."

The article went on to say that Skinner "… now has well over 150 hardy and beautiful originations to his credit; 240 introductions of ornamental plants from other parts of the world, plus 15 citations and awards, which in spite of his modesty, speak well for his efforts and success…monetary rewards are another thing, although this factor appears never to have disturbed Dr. Skinner or his work. He has worked completely independent of any government source."

Above: Harness makers were kept busy in Manitoba's fledgling towns.

The Russell Banner also reported that the award which gave Dr. Skinner his greatest pleasure was one he received from the citizens of Shellmouth Municipality, plus the mention of him in the *Encyclopaedia Canadiana* which lists a very limited number of living Canadians.

Unfortunately, the Dropmore of Frank Skinner's youth is gone. It succumbed to school consolidation, loss of the railway, bigger farm units and paved highways to larger centres. Although a robust community spirit continued to exist, the village itself was gradually deserted. Dr. Skinner died in 1967 but his legacy of hardy trees and hundreds of ornamental shrubs survived. Dropmore's place in history is assured by the genius of one of its first citizens.

EBOR

TRAVELLERS ON MANITOBA'S PROVINCIAL ROAD 255 just east of the Manitoba-Saskatchewan boundary easily pass the site of Ebor without knowing it. The village was born in 1904 when Isaac Heywood opened a store. It was soon followed by a second store, a livery barn, butcher shop, harness-maker, post office, poolroom and bowling alley, boarding house and other businesses that included three elevators.

The people of Ebor not only worked hard but, according to surviving accounts, were avidly interested in sports and many other kinds of recreation. To forward the sport interest, an Athletic Association was formed in 1908 with a membership fee of $1 a season. Out of this organization came teams for hockey, football, baseball and cricket.

A characteristic of community life not only in Ebor but most other pioneer settlements was that enthusiasm and originality frequently substituted for money. At the Association's second annual sports day, for instance, the football game had to be abandoned. The football burst and finances didn't permit a second ball to be held for an emergency. Since the game was scoreless, the prize money was divided between Ebor and a visiting team from nearby Comer.

These sports days were very popular and invariably followed by a dance. In fact, almost everything was followed by a dance. In 1914, the *Maryfield News* attested to the stamina of party-goers with this item: "We are pleased to report a very pleasant evening spent at Dad Heywood's room on Friday last. Everything went off well and dancing was kept up until four a.m. when everyone departed for home feeling they had thoroughly enjoyed themselves. The evening was sponsored by the Conversazione Club. Admission was free. Ladies brought lunch."

The *Maryfield News* and the *Reston Recorder* shared the task of reporting Ebor news. The only newspaper that Ebor ever had was in the early days when items of local interest were printed on a single sheet of paper. None seems to have survived, a not surprising consequence since the one copy per issue was nailed to the livery barn door for passers-by to peruse.

The other papers, however, were kept busy. The anxiety and sadness brought about by the great influenza epidemic, which killed millions of people after World War One, was revealed in a 1920 edition of the *Maryfield News*: "Had an earthquake occurred, it could not have been any more surprising to the combined district of Bardal and Ebor to learn with profound regret and sadness of the death of James Reynolds,

Opposite: A flock of chickens and turkeys meant food for the pioneer tables and sometimes a bit of cash for household needs.

Above: The front cover of a pamphlet published by the Manitoba Department of Agriculture in 1892. Glowing reports such as this one and similar optimistic advertising by the Dominion government attracted settlers by the tens of thousands, creating a host of new communities – and potential ghost towns.

Mrs. G. Peloquin and infant child. We understand the death of all three happened under one roof within hours of each other, the cause being flu and pneumonia."

Another concern surfaced after the Canadian Federal Prohibition Measure expired in 1919 and a huge rum-running trade to the United States began flourishing over a route just west of Ebor. The locals were kept informed of the unwelcome intrusion by the *Reston Recorder*. One issue in 1922 noted: "A booze car was seen passing through town on Monday evening at a high rate of speed. The drivers of these cars have no respect for public safety."

The two newspapers supplied residents with information regarding dances, concerts and community suppers, as well as weather and road conditions.

On October 31, 1929, the reporter who wrote the Ebor news portion of the *Reston Recorder* worried: "Snow which fell all day Monday and part of Tuesday has made the roads impassable for cars at present, but with mild weather traffic will soon be able to get through again. It is hoped the roads will again be fit for travel by Friday, the day the W.I. (Women's Institute) are holding their oyster and fowl supper and dance."

Nature co-operated, although barely, for in the following edition the paper reported: "The bazaar, fowl supper, concert and dance held in the hall last Friday evening under the auspices of the Women's Institute was well attended considering the condition of the roads and weather. About two hundred attended the supper. Some came a considerable distance, Ewart, Maryfield, Virden and other places sending representatives. About $100 was made clear of expenses."

Other events reported over the years were amateur stage productions, minstrel shows and the formation of a Literary Society. If these activities didn't satisfy the recreational needs of everyone, there were boxing matches, ping-pong, curling, bowling, billiards, snowshoeing, chess and croquinole parties. Much of the entertainment was shared by neighbouring villages and transportation was supplied, in part, by the "Peanut."

The nickname, for a reason lost in history, was given to the Reston-Wolseley line of the CPR which provided passenger and freight services to the villages between those points. Three cents a mile was the passenger rate. Sometimes even cheaper transportation was available when the handcar was used by the young people to get to a neighbouring village for a party.

The Orange Lodge played a large part in this Protestant community and their hall was used for church services by Anglicans, Presbyterians, and later the United Church. They all shared their ministers with other congregations. It was also used for many social events and as a high school before a two-roomed school was built.

Dedicated and hard-working women fostered most of the charitable, cultural and civic-minded projects by their membership and work in the Ebor Women's Institute. They raised money in a variety of ways to help pay for building the rink and the lighting plant, and then paying off the rink debt. Later, when hydro became available, they helped finance the re-wiring of the rink.

The Institute also maintained a travelling library in the early years as well as providing the residents with courses in first aid and home nursing, nutrition, sewing, home-management and similar activities. The tireless group also raised enough money during the latter years of the depression to have dental services provided for the school children.

At the height of Ebor's development a speculator purchased three acres of land adjoining the village, hoping to subdivide it into residential lots. But before his plan materialized the community had started to decline. The main reason was improved roads and the increasing number of trucks and automobiles that took residents to larger centres such as Virden and Reston. Ebor, like so many other small communities, languished by the wayside.

Although the old school, built in 1928, was still standing in the 1980s, little else remained of this once bustling village with its dedicated Women's Institute whose members worked so hard to better their community.

EWART

ALTHOUGH PRAIRIE TOWNS WERE BORN, FLOURISHED AND DIED with distressing frequency, not many were given a wake. In fact the community of Ewart is perhaps the only one which can claim this distinction.

Located 10 km (six miles) northwest of Reston, Ewart was born about 1901. Not until 1905, however, when the Reston-Wolseley line of the CPR was built did it begin significant development. Originally known as Bardal, then Haanel, it was renamed Ewart in honour of John Skirving Ewart, a well-known Manitoba lawyer and author. The first store and grain elevator were built in 1905 with other businesses gradually following. Also present was the optimism characteristic of the era. In 1912 the *Reston Recorder* noted: "Ewart, ever alive to the necessity of a growing town, has organized a Board of Trade. Membership fee is $1.00."

While pioneer optimism resulted in settlers overcoming an amazing variety of hardships, there were obstacles even optimism could not surmount. One was the massive depression of the 1930s. In addition to this calamity,

southern Manitoba had to contend with the added burden of crop-destroying drought and severe grasshopper plagues. An exception was 1935. That year crops were ruined by rust. Residents from more fortunate parts of the province endeavoured to assist, as a typical news item in the *Portage la Prairie Daily Graphic* reported: "Tentative arrangements were made at a mass meeting held on Tuesday night to send a car of vegetables to the dried out area of southern Manitoba…The carload of vegetables consists of 100 bushels of potatoes, cabbage, cucumbers, tomatoes, citron, pumpkin and squash…"

While this help was important, it didn't solve the problem of feeding the cattle. Many farmers were forced to move their herds to more northerly parts of the province such as Swan River, Bowsman and Dauphin where there was more abundant pasture.

Left: The pupils are now adults, Ewart's school is gone and the community nearly so.

Even if there had been crops to sell, prices of 8 cents a bushel for barley, 6 cents for oats and 25 for wheat wouldn't have made anyone rich. Although prices of the few "store-bought" necessities were correspondingly low, lack of cash made life difficult.

The hard times also adversely affected small wildlife, especially gophers and rabbits. Since gopher tails brought bounty of one cent each, the animals were enthusiastically hunted by children. Many rabbits suffered a similar fate. They were worth as much as 10 cents each, and though the capture required better organization than trapping gophers, "rabbit drives" became part of life.

The participants, spread out in a circle about one mile in diameter, beat the grass and bushes with sticks. This action drove the animals to a central location where they were caught in a snow-fence trap. Although the revenue derived was meagre, every penny was valuable and on one occasion went to pay the medical expenses of a sick child.

One valuable local asset was the community hall built in 1913. It was much used, with the Women's Institute – as they did in virtually every other settlement – sponsoring whist drives, dances and suppers. They provided courses in sewing, cooking, preserving and other household activities and acquired books from the Extension Library. The hall was also used as a place of worship. Services were held during the summer months and conducted, usually, by ministers from the Reston Anglican church.

Sports were an integral part of life in Ewart and there were many softball, baseball and tennis players. Curling also became popular after an ingenious plan enabled residents to build a rink. They could only afford the framework, which was constructed in 1912. Then they persuaded a local merchant, J.A. Smith, to loan enough lumber to cover the structure. In the spring the curlers carefully removed the lumber which Mr. Smith then put back into stock. In autumn, the process was repeated.

Joining the curling rink in a history that differed from the usual was the Pool elevator, built in 1926 by members of the Ewart Pool Elevator Association. It served the community until 1961 when the railway line was abandoned. In 1966 it was moved to Linklater, an event described by the *Reston Recorder.* "No, your eyes weren't deceiving you – that was a grain elevator parked on No. 2 Highway...

"The 180 ton, 80 ft. elevator, supported on equipment weighing 20 tons, completed its journey started two weeks ago, when the elevator was loaded and moved to the gravel road leading from Ewart to the No. 2 Highway. Soft roads stalled the move until Tuesday morning when the journey was resumed. Soft spots on the gravel road made the journey a slow one, as gravel reinforcing had to be hauled to several of the grades through the sloughs.

"Champagne Movers Ltd. of St. Norbert, contractors for the journey, used four trucks as motive power."

Linklater, however, was not the final home for this travelling elevator. It was moved again, this time across the border to Antler, Saskatchewan, to serve that community. During its travels it logged 34 km (21 miles), perhaps not enough to warrant inclusion in the *Guinness Book of Records* but fair mileage for a grain elevator.

The curling rink had a more humble ending. It was used for some years in its "on-in-the-fall, off-in-the-spring" configuration. But interest in curling waned, perhaps because of the twice annual construction bees, and the rink was abandoned. By 1946 interest in the sport had grown and money was raised to build a new one-sheet rink, this time with boards that didn't have to be removed in fall and spring. In 1948 it and the quarter-century old community hall were destroyed by a cyclone. The curling rink was replaced and used until 1969. Then the attraction of nearby Reston's artificial ice rink, linked by a good road, proved irresistible and Ewart's curlers went there for their games.

After the cyclone the community hall wasn't rebuilt, although part of it served the community for years afterward. During the cyclone, a box of dishes and a piano were hurled into a nearby slough. Both suffered only slight damage. After minor repairs, the piano gave many more years of service in a school, which was used later as a community centre.

The school is now gone and so, unfortunately, is Ewart, not because of lack of community spirit but a changing lifestyle that affected all of Canada. The consolidation of schools and churches, improved roads and transportation took people to larger centres to conduct their business. Also, a change from small to large farms reduced the rural population that once supported the small settlements.

But such was Ewart's community spirit that former residents expressed their esteem in a way that was as unique as their first curling rink. They organized a wake – or a "last supper" – in honour of their departed village. Assisted by $400 in assets from the former Ewart Curling Club, it was held in August 1975.

Some 450 people from coast to coast in Canada and as far south as California gathered for the party, which took place in Reston. So successful was this reunion that *Ewart Echoes*, a community history, was published. The foreword from the book reads, in part: "We made this effort for those attending the Ewart Community Reunion on August 3rd, 1975 and to provide a record of life around Ewart, a village which has almost disappeared."

Above: John Skirving Ewart, 1901, Manitoba lawyer and author.

Below: The Hartney Women's Institute in 1914.

GRAND VALLEY

Above, Right: The Coombs and Stewart Store in the early 1880s, was floated from Grand Valley and became the first store in Brandon.

JUST EAST of Brandon on Provincial Road 457 a fieldstone cairn marks the site of Grand Valley. It is all that remains of a community that died when a Scottish settler bargained with the railway – and lost.

In 1878 the McVicar brothers, Dougald and John, arrived in Winnipeg from Grenville, Quebec. With their belongings on their backs, they walked west, following the deep ruts left by oxcarts on the trail to Portage la Prairie. At that time the proposed route of the CPR's transcontinental railway ran north of Portage la Prairie toward Edmonton and the Yellowhead Pass. Since most settlers wanted land near a railway they turned northwest at Portage la Prairie. Not so the McVicars. They chose a more southerly course and eventually selected land on the Assiniboine River about 205 km (125 miles) west of Winnipeg.

Here, on the north bank of the river, they built a dugout home in the side of a hill and settled down to a somewhat solitary existence. There were few neighbours at first although Métis fur traders, accompanied by Aboriginals with ponies for sale, occasionally passed that way. The Métis, bound for Winnipeg from Qu'Appelle and Wood Mountain, guided strings of 100 or more Red River carts crammed with pemmican and furs. Dougald and John bought pemmican and buffalo meat from these travellers but for other supplies they had to return to Portage la Prairie or make the 35-km (21-mile) journey north to Rapid City.

During the winter of 1878-79 the McVicars contracted to cut logs at Riding Mountain for a sawmill in Rapid City. With some of the lumber they erected a two-storey house for the arrival of their wives and families that summer. By this time more settlers were moving into the area and Dougald McVicar saw the need for a post office. He applied to the Canadian government and was successful, with his wife appointed first postmistress.

The post office representative offered to immortalize the McVicar name by applying it to the new post office. But the family demurred. Mrs. McVicar, without seeing her new home, had already christened it Grand Valley. In a letter written years later Mrs. McVicar's daughter, Lillian, explained how the name was born: "(It) was suggested to her mind after reading an article written by the Rev. Thomas Lawson who with the Rev. Mr. Holstead of Portage la Prairie was wandering around one dark and rainy night and father, hearing their calls, went out with a lantern and brought them into his dugout…" McVicar gave them hot coffee and bannock, made a bed for them on the dugout floor and looked after their horses. "When writing about this, the Rev. Mr. Lawson referred to the 'Wonderful Valley' where they were treated so well."

During the fall and winter of 1879 the population of Grand Valley rose to nearly three dozen. Among the newcomers was Henry Foster of Halifax, who came west in response to glowing accounts sent by a relative at Grand Valley. Accompanied by his wife and children, he arrived at Winnipeg in October and made the remainder of the journey to Grand Valley by oxcart. One of his daughters later wrote: "We were three weeks on the road. The trails were so bad that we nearly always stuck in the mud just when we decided to camp for the night. We arrived at Grand Valley November 3, 1879… It was just at sunset and the smoky Brandon Hills, and the hills to the West…with the Assiniboine River winding through looked lovely. How often we would say 'Wouldn't it be nice to see lights on the hill across the river'."

Settlers continued to arrive by oxcart, on foot, or by river boat to the town that was quickly forming on the northeast corner of McVicar's land. By the summer of 1880 there were many tents and shacks, as well as several structures of logs or lumber. Businesses included six general stores, a jewellery store, harness shop, bakery and Dougald McVicar's brickyards. Brownlee's comfortable tent-hotel provided accommodation; there was a drug store and even a resident doctor. Traffic on the river was substantial, as was activity around the McVicar wharf and freight shed where goods were received for distribution to Rapid City and Tanner's Crossing (now Minnedosa). McVicar even built a ferry to replace the caulked wagon box once used to cross the river.

Speculators came, too, for railway engineers had appeared in Grand Valley and rumours were circulating about a change in the CPR's route. Sure enough, the railway had abandoned plans for their northern line to the Rockies and would cross the prairies through Grand Valley. The town was obviously destined to become the railway divisional point since it was the required distance from Winnipeg. The McVicars, once indifferent to a railway, changed their view. Early in 1881, as CPR surveyors marked out a road bed and river crossing, John McVicar arranged to have his land surveyed into lots.

By now the population had grown to 400. Lots were selling for an astronomical $2,000, and hammer

and saw kept pace with the quick exchange of money and land. The completion of each new house was celebrated with a dance and the future seemed as bright as a prairie sunrise. Unfortunately, this prosperity ended abruptly.

In April 1881, General Lafayette Rosser of the CPR arrived. Tall, handsome, and powerful, he made his offer – $25,000 for the townsite. McVicar wanted $50,000. Rosser turned and left, and as he strode away the fate of the town was decided. A little more than three km (two miles) west, on the south bank of the river, Rosser settled for property that became the railway divisional point. That community swiftly mushroomed into the city of Brandon.

The people of Grand Valley, however, had a more immediate problem. On June 22 the Assiniboine overflowed and surged through the town. Tents and shacks collapsed and floated away. A child was swept out of his house and down the road where his father miraculously managed to save him. But a young surveyor died and his body was removed by boat from the second storey of a house.

Many residents and merchants moved out. Coombs and Stewart floated their shanty-store to Brandon on a raft and became the first store in the new town. Others hung on, hoping that Grand Valley would somehow survive. In a show of optimism the following year a group of parents hired a teacher and opened a classroom above a store until a new school could be built on higher ground. The McVicars and other homesteaders belatedly signed away part interest in their lands in a desperate bid to secure a station and siding.

Sadly, trains did not stop at Grand Valley. Then in the summer of 1882, the Assiniboine flooded again. The remaining business people left, most of them for Brandon. Even Dougald McVicar eventually swallowed his chagrin and opened a brickyard in Brandon. The deserted townsite sold for $1,500. Brandon, by contrast, grew into Manitoba's second largest city.

Above: An 1890 pamphlet typical of many published to lure immigrants to the west.

IN APRIL 1881, GENERAL LAFAYETTE ROSSER OF THE CPR ARRIVED. TALL, HANDSOME, AND POWERFUL, HE MADE HIS OFFER – $25,000 FOR THE TOWNSITE.

GRANTOWN

THE TASTE OF PEMMICAN WASN'T WONDERFUL and it could be hard on the teeth. Some say it made for downright monotonous eating. But on the western plains during fur trade days it was just about the only food available. It was full of nutrition and lasted forever so what more could a hungry settler ask when crops failed from frost and flood or were eaten by grasshoppers?

Certainly, in 1824, the Red River settlers near the Forks (now Winnipeg) had pemmican on their minds when they welcomed the news of Cuthbert Grant's new village along the Assiniboine River. Not only would Grantown provide a buffer between them and the hostile Sioux, but its population of buffalo hunters could replenish the Colony's dwindling supply of 'plains provisions' or dried buffalo meat and pemmican.

The French-speaking Métis of Grantown, proud, daring warriors and hunters, were mixed-blood descendants of French voyageurs and native women. Their leader, Cuthbert Grant, was himself the product of a *marriage du pays* (country marriage), for there were no clergy in the west then to do the honours. His father, also Cuthbert Grant, a Scot, was a trader and partner in the North West Company; his mother, whose name is unknown, was a mixed-blood Cree. Although Grant spoke English, through his father and his own education in Scotland, he

CUTHBERT GRANT 1793-1854

Son of a Scots trader and an Indian mother, Grant became a clerk in the North West Company and leader of the Métis in their struggle against the Selkirk Settlement and the Hudson's Bay Company. In 1816 he led the party which killed Governor Semple and his followers at Seven Oaks and captured Fort Douglas; but after 1821 he became reconciled with the colony. The Company named him "Warden of the Plains", and charged him with keeping order on the southern prairies. In 1839 he became a Councillor of Assiniboia and magistrate, capping a life dedicated to the native people of the West.

Fils d'un commerçant écossais et d'une mère indienne, Grant fut commis de la Compagnie du Nord-Ouest et dirigea la lutte des Métis contre la colonie de Selkirk et la Compagnie de la Baie d'Hudson. Au cours de l'affrontement des Sept-Chênes, en 1816, sa troupe extermina celle du gouverneur Semple et s'empara du fort Douglas. Après la fusion des deux compagnies en 1821, il devint «surveillant des Plaines» avec mission de maintenir l'ordre dans les prairies du sud. En 1839, il fut nommé magistrat et conseiller de l'Assiniboia, ce qui couronnait toute une vie consacrée aux autochtones de l'Ouest.

Historic Sites and Monuments Board of Canada.
Commission des lieux et monuments historiques du Canada.

Government of Canada - 1975 - Gouvernement du Canada

was also at home with French learned from his mother. No doubt he used Michif when needed, a Métis dialect resulting from the influence of various native tongues on the French language.

Grant had been named "Captain General of all the Métis in the Country" in the spring of 1816 by virtue of his connection to and affection for these *bois-brûlés* who were just beginning to see themselves as a new nation. At that time, like his father before him, Grant served the North West Company with whole-hearted loyalty. However, his employer's suspicion of the Hudson's Bay Company and its motives in establishing a settlement at Red River — across the North West Company's traditional supply route to its own far-flung posts — led to disastrous results.

Foremost among these calamities was the tragic confrontation at Seven Oaks in June 1816, during which Grant and several of his followers routed and killed Governor Semple and twenty of his men. Grant was

charged with the murder of Semple although his was not the hand that took his life. In fact, some witnesses claimed that he did his utmost to calm the hot-headed Métis, wheeling his horse in front of them and ordering them to stop.

In any case, the murder charge did not stick and, in spite of his somewhat turbulent history up to that point, Grant is credited with eventually bringing about peaceful settlement. He turned many of the Métis from their nomadic life and hostility toward the settlers of Red River to a new role as their defenders and providers. Historian Margaret Arnett Macleod wrote that following this accomplishment, "…he increasingly gained in public esteem and served with honour in responsible positions."

When the North West Company united with the Hudson's Bay Company in 1821, Grant served a brief stint as a clerk of the HBC at Fort Garry. But in 1824, he was forced to retire from the Company due to interference from colonists who could not forget his role in the disturbances. Governor George Simpson then devised a plan whereby Grant could form a Métis settlement. Some say that the Governor, for reasons of his own, had this plan in mind all along. Whatever the case, Grant was agreeable to it. The previous year, in St. Boniface Cathedral, he had married Marie McGillis, mixed-blood daughter of Angus McGillis, and was already thinking of becoming a settler with his new father-in-law.

By this time, the merger of the two fur companies had displaced many of the Métis from their jobs as voyageurs and cart drivers. While some of them had moved to the Red River settlement, others settled at Pembina, a dangerous location in the view of the Hudson's Bay Company and others. Part of this danger, in addition to increasing attacks from the Sioux, was the Company's fear of losing trade furs to American dealers. The Company closed the post, throwing more Métis out of work.

Simpson hoped that Grant's new settlement would relieve some of the problems created by these events and in that he proved correct. In a letter to Andrew Colville, dated May 31, 1824, Simpson reported that Grant and his father-in-law were joined by about 80 Métis men, all married with families.

Simpson had given Cuthbert Grant a piece of land six miles long and six miles in depth along the Assiniboine River. Grant divided it into river lots, keeping the central ones for himself and for a church and distributing those on either side to family and to the best warriors and buffalo hunters. His interest in the Catholic faith of his followers had grown with his marriage to Marie McGillis and he continued, as a new Catholic, to support the Church throughout his life.

About this time, too, Governor Simpson managed to procure from William McGillivray, Grant's inheritance of possibly £14,000, which had been left to him as a young boy when his father died. As Grant's guardian, McGillivray had sent him, according to his father's wishes, to be educated in Scotland. When Grant returned,

Above: A Métis cottage, 1870.

Below: Cuthbert Grant, founder of Grantown.

Above: A gravestone in the cemetery at St. Francois Xavier.

THE MARKSMEN GALLOPED THROUGH THIS SNORTING, THUNDERING MELEE, FIRING AND RELOADING THEIR MUSKETS, RISKING LIFE AND LIMB TO BRING DOWN THE GREAT BEASTS.

ready and willing to work in the North West Company, McGillivray continued for a time to look after his interests. Now Governor Simpson would take over that role.

So it was a happily married and moderately well-to-do Cuthbert Grant who gave his name to Grantown and set about to lead his "young fellows," the Métis, in the ways of settlement. He began by gradually clearing nearly fifty acres of his own land, the other settlers following his lead. By 1832, using only hand ploughs, they had cultivated 298 acres and six years later that number had almost tripled.

Life for the Métis in Grantown, though, was not all farming for there was always the hunt. They needed pemmican and indeed were expected by the Hudson's Bay Company to produce it, not only to feed their own families but to sell to the Company and to the hard-pressed settlers at the Forks.

The Métis were happy to oblige. Each June and in the fall, they set forth with the captain of the hunt, usually Cuthbert Grant, to find the buffalo. Only the disabled and the very young or old were left at the village. Women and children rode the creaking carts or walked alongside the mounted hunters as they moved off across the White Horse Plain. Hunters from Red River joined them for a rendezvous at Pembina Crossing with another party of Métis hunters from Pembina. Onward they went, to wherever the distant, hulking shapes of buffalo could be sighted. Accompanying them was a chaplain who would say Mass for them, for the Métis were a devout people and kept the Sabbath holy, even out on the plains in the midst of a hunt.

The hunt was a disciplined affair, organized by Grant along military lines, which served them well in warfare with the Sioux, on whose hunting grounds they encroached. If warned by scouts of imminent attack, the Métis quickly placed the carts, shafts up and forward, in a circle around their women, children and livestock. Then they prepared to fire from hastily scooped rifle pits in front. Often the circles of carts were reinforced and stabilized with poles, ropes and other objects.

When a herd of buffalo was discovered, the Métis pitched camp in a similar large circle, tents at one end and livestock at the other. Then off rode the hunters on finely trained ponies to run the buffalo. Alexander Ross, in an eye-witness account of a 1840 hunt related how the earth trembled when the horses started out but when the buffalo fled, "it was like the shock of an earthquake."

The marksmen galloped through this snorting, thundering melee, firing and reloading their muskets, risking life and limb to bring down the great beasts. When the killing ceased, the camp moved up with the carts and the women began to dress the meat, or as much of it as they could save in the summer heat. They particularly craved the tongues, a delicacy that could be pickled in brine.

After a feast of fresh meat, the women cut the remainder into strips to be dried over poles in the sun. Then they pounded the dried meat into powder and mixed it with melted fat in sacks of new buffalo hide. In summer they added berries picked on the prairie. The hunt continued in this manner until the hundreds of carts were filled, each one carrying between 500 and 1,000 pounds of dried meat, pemmican and hides.

Grant always enjoyed the hunt and so, apparently, did his brother-in-law, Pierre Falcon, Bard of the Prairie, who wrote a song about the stampeding herds, their sharp horns and the brave bois-brûlés who hunted them down. Falcon's songs enlivened many an evening at Grantown and were sung in the canoes by voyageurs, who paddled thousands of miles in the service of the Company. No doubt, as the songs entertained these wilderness men they also helped maintain the rhythm of their paddle-strokes.

Another activity enjoyed by the young and old of Grantown was sugar-making in the early spring when families travelled as far as thirty miles to the best sugar-maple stands at what is now called the Boyne River. These were Manitoba maples, which produced a different-tasting syrup from that of the more familiar sugar maple of eastern Canada.

The women of Grantown prepared for the sugar making well in advance. They harvested birch bark and stored it in sheds until winter. Then, they fashioned bark vessels of various shapes and sizes in which to collect the syrup and store the sugar. In fact, this became one of their principal crafts.

Not to be outdone, the men of Grantown became famous for their well-crafted Red River carts. The carts were especially noted for the deeply-dished wheels which made for good balance on the rough terrain of the prairie.

So the little village on the Assiniboine was becoming an active and well-known community. It was a good stopping place for travellers going west or east, many of whom found hospitality in Grant's own home. Others camped nearby, knowing that Grant kept a good supply of provisions on hand for those in need of replenishing their own goods. The town became a trading post when Grant, under a special licence, worked as a trader.

In the first years of settlement, Grant had built a water-mill on Sturgeon Creek to grind the settlers' wheat. As it was not entirely successful, he erected a windmill right at the village. Meanwhile, the village grew, with whitewashed homes along the riverbank and Grant's spacious white home in the centre of it all. There was a trading post and blacksmith shop and, in time, schooling was provided for the children, at first in Grant's home. Later, when two Grey Nuns came to live at the village in 1850 their convent-school immediately attracted eighty pupils.

The first church in Grantown was built of poles in 1828 and stood next to Grant's home as he had arranged. That same year Grant was appointed "Warden of the Plains of Red River" by the Council of the Northern Department of Rupertsland, with orders to prevent illicit trade in furs in the area. For this he received a salary of £200 per annum. Later, in 1835, he was made Justice of the Peace for White Horse Plain and became a sheriff of Assiniboia in 1837.

In 1832, a start was made on a new church to replace the earlier, rather flimsy structure. Its first Mass took place on Christmas Eve 1833 and the church registry was begun the following year. The parish, a mission of St. Boniface until then, had been given the name St. Francois Xavier. There were 424 parishioners, a number that grew to 900 in Grant's lifetime.

In 1849 Grant's appointment as Warden of the Plains was not renewed after a farcical trial of four Métis who had defied the Company's monopoly in the fur trade. Two of the accused were Grant's neighbours, one of them his wife's brother. A verdict of guilty against Guillaume Sayer, the first man tried, followed by his release without penalty was taken to mean 'not guilty' by the large crowd of angry and armed Métis outside. The Métis gave a triumphant yell, and believing that they were now free to trade without penalty, proceeded to do so. This event effectively ended any attempt to enforce the Hudson's Bay Company's despised monopoly through the court.

Grant's influence over his "young fellows" was fading, as Governor Simpson was quick to note. Grant continued as sheriff, however, and in 1850 became president of a quarterly petty court which met in his home.

In 1853 he was negotiating by letter with Governor Simpson to resume his life as a licensed free trader. But after a fall from a horse, his health declined and he died on July 15, 1854 at age 61. He was buried the next day with sorrow and with all the honour his neighbours and his church could give him. Under the altar of the hand-hewn church, consecrated at Grantown 21 years before, his body was laid to rest.

Before long the name Grantown faded away, replaced by the name of the parish of St. Francois Xavier. The herds of buffalo dwindled until they disappeared entirely from the western plains. Civilization encroached, bringing new industry, new people and new homes. The need for pemmican was gone and only a few remembered the songs, the scent of campfires and the whitewashed village along the river.

Above: St. Francois Xavier Church

HECLA

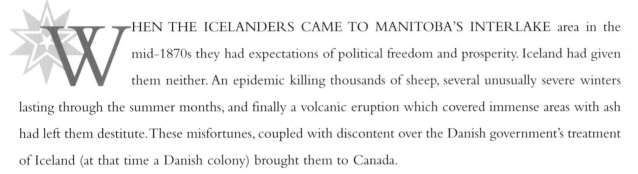HEN THE ICELANDERS CAME TO MANITOBA'S INTERLAKE area in the mid-1870s they had expectations of political freedom and prosperity. Iceland had given them neither. An epidemic killing thousands of sheep, several unusually severe winters lasting through the summer months, and finally a volcanic eruption which covered immense areas with ash had left them destitute. These misfortunes, coupled with discontent over the Danish government's treatment of Iceland (at that time a Danish colony) brought them to Canada.

The Interlake area, chosen partly for its similarity to their native land, seemed ideal for their purposes. Forests rich in spruce, balsam and pine; land for grazing cattle; the fertile waters of Lake Winnipeg teeming with whitefish, pickerel, pike and sauger promised unlimited commercial opportunity for the settlers and their descendants. Moreover, the Canadian government gave them exclusive settlement rights to an area on the west side of Lake Winnipeg six townships long and extending 20 km (12 miles) inland. This was land sufficient to ensure continued immigration from Iceland for many years. Unfortunately New Iceland, as they called their chosen home, proved little more hospitable than the old.

The first settlers arrived in 1875, nearly 300 Icelanders from eastern Ontario and Wisconsin under the guidance of Sigtyggur Jonasson and John Taylor, an Englishman who befriended them. Another 1,226 arrived from Iceland in 1876 and 220 more in 1878. The colony was unique in that it was responsible only to the federal government since it was, at first, beyond the borders of Manitoba. It was, in effect, a miniature republic with its own constitution and political system. In 1881, when the boundary of Manitoba was extended north to the 53rd parallel, it became part of the province but was allowed to continue with its own government for another six years.

Included in the Icelandic Reserve was 15,715-ha (38,000-acre) Hecla Island off the west shore of Lake Winnipeg. Here, a group of thirty-one families took up homesteads in 1876. Previously known as Big Island, it was called Mikley, or Magnificent, Island by the Icelanders. It did not live up to its nickname, and eventually came to be called Hecla for a volcano that spewed destruction in Iceland.

During the first few years Hecla Island yielded the settlers only hardship, sickness and death. Even hopes of employment at the Island's sawmill died when the owner (who also owned the store) refused to hire Icelanders.

Opposite: The decline of the commercial fishing industry on Lake Winnipeg, foreshadowed the decline of Hecla Village.

Later, when the mill owner married an Icelandic girl, his attitude changed and he taught the Icelanders how to fish through the ice – a skill he had learned from the Aboriginals. This knowledge saved many from starvation during the first terrible winter of 1876-77, a time recalled by settler Sigurour Erlendson in *Mikley The Magnificent Island* by I.S. McKillip: "…there was more snow that winter than ever again in my time. My son Stefan, now twelve, and I had to trudge in favourable weather through snow reaching up to our thighs searching for wood to chop and carry home." The owner of the mill loaned Erlendson a hut which, although poor in shape, helped the family survive. "There was a clay stove in one corner but no chimney to or through the roof…we were most often choking from smoke or shivering from cold."

Erlendson's neighbours also knew hardship, some even spending the long bitter winter in tents. To add to their misery and grief, about half the population contracted smallpox and 30 out of the 140 settlers died.

Nevertheless, they stayed and in 1877 wrote the government asking that their Island be properly surveyed and that the settlement on the east side be divided "…to leave each lot only 20 chains wide…extending as far back from the shore as is required to have them contain 160 acres each." Thus began the village of Hecla.

The Icelander's respect for God and education made church and school priorities. At first both were held in settlers' homes, with school enrollment large because adults also attended. Sometimes they sat on the step or even on the woodpile with their books. By 1880 a proper one-room school was ready.

Religious affairs went much less smoothly. In 1877 Reverend Jon Bjarnason, who had received his training in the rather liberal Lutheran church in Iceland, held the first church service at Hecla. Plans were soon begun to build a church. The next year, however, the settlement was visited by Reverend Pall Thorlakson who had been ordained by the Norwegian Lutheran Synod in Missouri which embraced more fundamentalist beliefs.

Loyalties were divided and the resulting rift was the main factor in the subsequent large migration in 1878 from New Iceland to Southern Manitoba and the United States. Another factor was that the Icelanders could see little hope for improvement in their living standards. They had no fish or cattle to sell and there was no market for wood. Of the twenty-six homesteads taken up, eighteen were abandoned.

Because of the exodus it wasn't until 1890 that the community was able to complete its own church, the first in New Iceland. By now there had been more immigration from Iceland and a fishing industry was slowly developing. A major problem was that taking the fish to Winnipeg involved a trek with oxen of 177 km (110 miles) each way on poor roads in bitterly cold weather.

The Icelander's respect for God and education made church and school priorities.

The fishing itself was as arduous as the long trip to Winnipeg. Except for spring break-up, it was a year-round occupation. When the water was open, the men set nets in the lake and rowed to the sites in flat-bottomed skiffs. But when the lake was frozen, dogs were used to haul food, equipment and fish to a camp, which had been established the previous fall. That camp, often just a small shack, became home for the fishermen until the season was over.

The fish that were not needed for home consumption were sold to fish companies. The fishermen usually were not fairly paid for their catches since the companies did not quote prices until the season was far enough advanced to determine the catch. Then they would all make the same quote. A local co-op failed to improve prices paid fishermen for their arduous work. Not until 1958 did the Manitoba Federation of Fishermen establish a Fish Marketing Board and assure fairer prices.

More problems loomed ahead, though, for the struggling community. In the 1960s mercury was found in some species and commercial fishing on Lake Winnipeg was stopped. The Federation of Fishermen was instrumental in getting compensation for the men, but when the lake reopened the provincial government placed a limit on the number of licenses issued and fish taken. The decline of the fishing industry foreshadowed the decline of Hecla Village.

During the years when fishing had been the community's main means of support – frail though it was – other industries were present. A number of sawmills were in operation over the years and pulpwood was exported in winter over the ice. Limestone was mined and barged to Winnipeg; a mink ranch, several stores, a garage, and other businesses were established. Unfortunately, all failed.

In addition to the difficulties of finding a viable industrial base, island residents – the population rose to a peak of some 500 in the 1930s – lacked proper medical facilities. There were midwives and a self-trained doctor, Johann Straumfjord, who ministered to their needs. But he wasn't readily accessible since he lived on a small island northwest of Hecla. The nearest qualified doctor was 40 km (25 miles) away at Riverton on the mainland.

Trips to Riverton were often risky across rough water or treacherous ice in blizzard conditions. During spring break-up and fall freeze-up they couldn't be made at all. Not only that, but doctors were expensive and a trip to one was undertaken only after serious consideration. To counter this drawback, in 1950 residents formed a unique organization called Help in Emergency. Its purpose was to offset medical costs with

Left: Heclingers hauled logs and field rocks and built hydro caissons to bring electricity to the island.

Above: Back from winter fishing.

Below: This abandoned boat once was part of a thriving industry at Hecla.

funds raised from members' fees as well as proceeds from social events such as dances and concerts.

Heclingers had over the generations shown their initiative and resourcefulness in other ways. Winter transportation needs spurred Dori Sigurgeirsson to invent his version of a snowmobile in 1920, long before such vehicles were built commercially. He used a Model T Ford and put tracks on the rear wheels while mounting the front of the rig on a sled. He also invented a device for setting nets by adapting the design of a hydraulic powered net drum used in West Coast fishing to winter fishing on Lake Winnipeg.

In 1953, a ferry provided the first regular connection with the mainland, but in order to link up with it, a road had to be built across the 10 km (6 miles) wide island to the west narrows. The men of Hecla donated both money and manual labour for the project. Then, when it seemed that they were to be denied hydro power because the government considered it impossible to construct a crib sufficiently sturdy to withstand the ice that passed through the narrows, Heclingers again took the initiative. They not only drew up the plans themselves, but did the actual construction, cutting

and hauling logs and field rock for the project. By late 1953 because of their work and initiative, electricity came to Hecla.

But even hard work and resourcefulness is no guarantee of survival in an inhospitable environment. When the old way of life began to disappear along with the fishing business, Islanders placed their last hope in tourism. Since the turn of the century Hecla had been popular with vacationers and many had built summer homes at Gull Harbour, 8 km (5 miles) northeast of Hecla Village. This beautiful harbour with 3 km (2 miles) of sandy beach increased in popularity over the years. So, to promote and increase recreational facilities, island residents formed their own development association.

In 1967, when the Manitoba government's Fund For Rural Development agreed to spend $85 million in the Interlake area, the future looked bright. A study was made and contained a plan to establish a provincial park. Another recommendation suggested: "Period buildings having a distinctive character and presently scattered all over the island, should be brought together to form the core of an historic village…Local population should be encouraged to continue living in these buildings, to dress

in period or ethnic costumes and to run the different businesses in the village." The park, comprising eight other islands in addition to Hecla, was to be opened in 1973.

In spite of such recommendations, however, the islanders soon discovered that it was not park policy to allow private ownership of lands within a park. The crown was to have it all.

In order to placate the owners, the government offered a lifetime lease-back for any wishing to remain. They also offered job opportunities and better incomes. For reasons not made clear, however, the lease-back offer was callously withdrawn and Heclingers told they had to leave.

Resentment was understandably deep. It deepened even more as expropriation proceeded. Residents protested that they were not being offered enough money for their property to enable them to relocate. As a result, an expropriation inquiry was held. One submission made to the inquiry by life-long residents Mr. and Mrs. Helgi Tomasson read, in part: "If we go we want replacement value. The government is trying to ruin us. I can't commute back and forth. Here I'm able to drive off the lake in my snowmobile, go right into my yard and my wife has dinner waiting for me. If I leave the island my fishing is done. I'd have nothing but hardship."

Many others testified at the hearings, including William Speechly who spoke on behalf of the summer residents: "If this group is sacrificed to the Crown's administrative convenience, and to the steam roller of tourism, then my enthusiasm for Canada and Manitoba will evaporate."

The government eventually came up with a proposal acceptable to the majority but there was dissension and resentment among the once cohesive group. Because the amount of payment for properties was public knowledge, comparisons were made and many were upset by what they considered to be unfair payments. But the antagonism between the residents and some

departments of the government was even greater. So much so that when the Parks Branch attempted to collect artifacts from the villagers for a museum, none was forthcoming.

Without co-operation from the people, the government abandoned its plan to restore the village. Instead it spent lavish sums on a 3-km (2-mile) long causeway, a navigation channel and bridge to replace the ferry. Also included were funds for a golf course, tennis courts, camping area, irrigation, sewage and road systems, parking lots, trails, nature programs and, later, a year round resort hotel at Gull Harbour.

In his report of the Hecla Island Expropriation Inquiry, Inquiry Officer J.S. Walker said: "In the process of dealing with the objections, it is evident that this report deals with the end of an era and the latter days of settlement on Hecla." His statement proved prophetic. By 1975, all that remained of the old village was the post office and general store, kept in business by tourists. At that time, the store was selling T-shirts printed with the question: "Is the Heclinger an Endangered Species?"

The answer appeared to be yes, since by 1981, only four of the original families remained on the Island and no effort had been made to reverse the situation. As noted in the inquiry report: "The Islanders stood on the sidelines forgotten...They became the least matter of concern in the park development program."

Since that time, however, the Islander's concerns have been addressed and original owners or their descendants given permission to purchase back their five acre holdings for $1,000 per acre. Starting in the late 1990s, many took advantage of the new ruling and now new homes as well as refurbished older ones line the beautiful beach at Hecla Island Village – almost all proudly flying the elegant red and blue Icelandic flag in addition to the Maple Leaf. The population is almost exclusively a summertime one, so its ghost town status applies only during the winter months.

Above: One of the challenges of opening the country was building and linking roadways. Here, road construction workers take a lunch break.

ISABELLA

**WE HAD THE
RAILWAY AND THE
START OF A TOWN
BUT NO FACILITIES
FOR HANDLING
THE GRAIN, NOT
EVEN A LOADING
PLATFORM.**

"THE CLIMATE OF MANITOBA CONSISTS OF SEVEN MONTHS of Arctic weather and five months of cold weather." This unflattering description of the province was printed in 1882 in the *Settlers' Guide to The North-West* published by the Northern Pacific Railway Company. In spite of the warning, however, optimistic settlers flocked westward to the fertile virgin prairie.

Those whose destination was an area which later became known as Isabella found that the railway ended at Brandon. To proceed further northwest required a long and sometimes hazardous trip up the winding Assiniboine River by sternwheel steamer to Fort Ellice Landing, Doyle's Landing or Herkemer's Landing. Then followed a trek of at least 40 km (25 miles) in Red River carts or horse and buggy over prairie trails established and still used by the Aboriginals. The Sioux Trail was one. Although the Sioux didn't make the settlers feel particularly welcome, there was no open hostility.

Another frequently used trail had a much different origin. Known as the Old Boiler Trail, it had been etched on the prairie during transportation of a huge boiler from a landing on the Assiniboine to Elphinstone, about 115 km (72 miles) northwest of Brandon. The boiler was intended for either a sawmill or gristmill and was massive. According to some early residents, it had to be pulled by 100 teams of horses and mules, its journey resulting in a well-defined trail. Ironically, the boiler was never used. During the journey it overbalanced and rolled down a hill.

Over the years settlement of the Isabella district continued but it was nearly a quarter of a century before construction of a school and post office signalled the birth of a town. According to the reminiscences of Mr. William Palmer, an early resident: "...when we got the post office, it was named after Mrs. Taylor, whose first name was Isabella. Likewise the name of the school and the town."

Soon after, in 1909, the farmers were glad to have the Canadian Northern Railway arrive since they had been hauling their grain to Birtle, Hamiota, Arrow River or Miniota. Marketing grain was not an easy task, as Mr. Palmer relates: "We had the railway and the start of a town but no facilities for handling the grain, not even a loading platform. It so happened that J.L. Thompson, a farmer west of town, had an elevating grain loader run by horse power. I borrowed this elevator and loaded 2 cars of wheat of my own and 3 other cars for neighbours....At that time the railway provided cars that carried a maximum of 1,100 bushels – 1,000 bushels plus 10%. There were other farmers who loaded their grain direct from the wagon into the car. This was not an easy job. The next year the Western Canada Flour Mills built an elevator and I was put in charge of it as agent. Green and inexperienced, I had a good many headaches."

Soon two more elevators were built and the Royal Crown Bank started operations, at first in a tent but then in space rented in the new hardware store. Other buildings and businesses included a school, church, ice-cream parlour, café, blacksmith shop, machine shop and implement agencies.

Minutes of a Board of Trade meeting held in 1911 illustrate the co-operative spirit in the growing community: "Mr. Scott then addressed the meeting at some length and stated in a fair manly way how he intended to do business....We will work hand in hand with him for the upbuilding of Isabella, and that when his goods arrive here we will volunteer to transfer them from the car to the store."

Mr. Palmer, who was still employed as elevator agent, acquired the agency for John Deere, International Harvester, Case Machinery and McLaughlin buggies. He also had a rural mail route and two school vans. As if these enterprises were not enough to fill his time, he foresaw and met another need.

"Our town, though not very large, was attracting Commercial travellers," he wrote, "and in order to accommodate the travelling public, we opened up our house as a boarding house to give meals and lodging." The business flourished and "...we could not accom-modate all the people...so I erected an addition to the house in 1915."

By now World War One had been in progress for over a year, causing the economic situation to fluctuate. "The implement business slowed down considerably but the price of all grains went up," Mr. Palmer wrote. "I can recall paying Will Taylor $3.65 a bushel for a car-lot of No.1 wheat....While the price of grain was good, many farmers increased their land holdings, instead of paying their debts, and I felt this quite keenly in my business." By 1918 Palmer had had enough and he closed his implement business and boarding house and left.

But others stayed and a strong community spirit developed. Organizations such as the Women's Institute contributed to the culture of the town and surrounding area by supporting music and drama festivals and a horticultural society. They also provided health care and home-making courses, but their biggest project was building a rink. They not only canvassed for funds but assumed the final payment of $700.

A Community Club organized an agricultural society, a fair and in 1951 built a community hall. Unfortunately, the spirit of co-operation couldn't save a town doomed by the consolidation of schools and the loss of the railway in the 1970s. Community pride remained and for a time area residents continued to use the church, rink, post office and store. But the Isabella of pioneer recollections is gone.

Above: A link to Isabella's pioneer past is the United Church built in 1911.

Below: Fort Ellice in1879. From this lonely outpost on the Assiniboine River settlers to the Isabella region still had to trek up to 40 km (25 miles) and wait nearly twenty-five years for a post office.

MAKINAK

MAKINAK IS AN ABORIGINAL WORD said by some sources to mean "good trail," while others believe it comes from the Cree "mikinak," meaning turtle. In one respect the difference of opinion really doesn't matter since the community incorporated both definitions. It was built on a gravelly ridge, once part of an old Aboriginal trail, about 10 km (6 miles) west of the Turtle River.

Like many frontier communities it had two locations, the first about one kilometre to the east, but when the Canadian Northern Railway was built through Neepawa to Dauphin in 1896 the hamlet moved to the railway tracks. It became a debarkation point for the tide of settlers moving into the trackless area to the east and to the north between Lake Dauphin and Lake Manitoba. As such it soon grew to be a typical frontier town.

A boxcar became the first railway station and along Main Street false-fronted and verandahed shops vied for trade. Business places included a blacksmith shop, livery barn, barbershop-poolroom and two boarding houses. About 1900 Dr. William Mason opened an office, and in 1904 a travelling missionary wrote that Makinak had "five or six stores" and the merchants were "a fine lot of fellows…working splendidly together." Makinak's future seemed assured.

Farmers from Rorketon, 45 km (28 miles) away, and from Ste. Rose du Lac and Ste. Amelie brought their grain and cattle to Makinak for shipment. From Riding Mountain came lumber, railway ties and cordwood, and from widely dispersed dairy herds came milk for Makinak's creamery, one of the first in the northern part of the province.

A link to this pioneer enterprise was former resident C.L. D'Aoust who spent his boyhood in the Makinak area and often worked in the creamery during school holidays. His work day began at 4 a.m. and when the teams started arriving at eight o'clock he would already have made 500 pounds of butter.

In addition to the creamery, D'Aoust remembered the frame schoolhouse built in 1898. "It was an iceberg," he said in an interview some years ago. "We'd sit around the stove and read our lessons and shiver. But I learned to read and write in both French and English there."

Opposite: The poolroom was an important place in pioneer communities. Makinak's in 1910 had uninsulated walls and a lantern ready above the player at left.

Left: Waiting for the train at Makinak in 1915, a scene common throughout the prairies for many decades.

MAKINAK. MAN. ÉTÉ.

...PIONEER BILL RUDD RECALLED THAT IN 1909 WHEN HE HELPED HIS FATHER MOVE TO MAKINAK, HE THOUGHT THE VILLAGE WAS THE END OF THE WORLD.

Above: Makinak's main street in 1930, before it was destroyed in a fire later that year.

Centre: Two youthful fiddlers demonstrate their skills.

A schoolboy's attention, however, was easily diverted from chalk dust and grammar books to the world outside the one-room school. Over at the railway tracks in autumn "the farmers would be lined up for about a mile with their grain," D'Aoust recalled, "some in bags, some loose in the wagon box." There were four elevators at Makinak with D'Aoust's father one of the elevator men. Competition for the grain was brisk, with buyers bidding against each other. This bidding, however, was not without risk and D'Aoust's father once had a month's wages docked to cover an over payment.

In the early 1900s, Makinak bustled winter and summer. As a result the village attracted more than the usual small town businesses. At one time or another it boasted a taxidermist, a metal plating works, a cement block factory, and a photographer, Anatole D'Aoust, C.L. D'Aoust's cousin.

Anatole was remembered by his cousin not only as a competent photographer but also as a gifted musician who "played the piano, organ, violin, and auto-harp." During the summer his studio was a tent as he roamed the countryside.

Included in his excellent collection which depicts a country in the making are photographs of the huge dredges used to dig drainage ditches in the low, boggy land around Makinak. Until the ditches were built about 1912, cross-country travel was a risky undertaking, best attempted by the nimble-footed or left until freeze up. In the district history, *Between Mountains and Lake*, published by the Ochre River Women's Institute, an early settler told of crossing a marsh in summertime by stepping from one willow clump to another: "If one fell off one would go over one's head in mud and water. My dad (John Price) often had to tie tea on the back of his neck to keep it dry until he got across."

In the same book pioneer Bill Rudd recalled that in 1909 when he helped his father move to Makinak, he thought the village was the end of the world. "(It was) surrounded by bush, water, and stumps," he recalled, with the road leading to the village "a muddy trail of stumps and water-filled holes."

The bleakness of the landscape, however, was softened by touches of beauty: patches of spring crocus, autumn's red Indian paintbrush, winter's wind-carved

snow. On cold winter nights the northern lights swished across Makinak skies in a display more brilliant, residents boasted, than at Churchill nearly 1,000 km (600 miles) to the north.

Into this austere and awesome land in 1897 came a shipload of orphan boys from England. They travelled under the care of Father Douglas, a Roman Catholic priest who was also an English lord. He intended to establish the boys in St. Joseph's Farm Home built that year on a 960 acre land grant near Makinak. Here, Father Douglas hoped, the orphans would learn the practical aspects of farming in preparation for taking up land of their own.

It was an ambitious and charitable project but it was not a success. After four years of struggle with poor soil and marketing problems, Father Douglas placed the boys in private homes and returned to England. Subsequent attempts by other clergy also failed and in 1912 the home was relocated south of Winnipeg.

Nevertheless, St. Joseph's Farm Home left a lasting impression on the people of Makinak. Some of them recall the Angelus bell each morning, noon and evening ringing an invitation to prayer. But more tangible than memories has been the presence in Makinak of succeeding generations of the George Mason family.

Mason, the only one of Father Douglas' boys who stayed in Makinak, worked for a time in Jack Campbell's store but by 1920 had opened a general store of his own. It is still in the family, operated by his son, Bill.

Above the store is a museum started in 1967 by the late Denis Mason, grandson of George. He started his collection of Makinak memorabilia as a centennial project and his parents, Rose and Bill, have continued in his memory. The building itself, erected about 1911, is the last remaining of the original structures along Main Street. The others were destroyed in 1930 by a fire that levelled most of Makinak's business section.

"Our store was saved by the fact that a fifty-foot vacant lot separated it from the burning buildings," Bill Mason explains. "The fire started about two o'clock in the morning in the loft of a livery barn on Main Street. The train crew spotted it when they stopped at the station to pick up the mail and they blew the train whistle and kept blowing it until the town woke up.

"The fire burned east at first," Mason recalls. "Then the wind changed and it burned west. Everyone turned out to help but when we ran out of water there wasn't much we could do."

The devastation was a death sentence because the town had been declining since 1912. That year the railway built a branch line to Ste. Rose du Lac, siphoning off much of Makinak's rail and grain trade. In an ironic turn of events, however, the town's elevator later enjoyed a revival of business because of closures in other villages. For a time, things looked good. Sales of farm supplies rose and, in 1980, a seed cleaning plant was opened.

But the boom didn't last. Today, the elevator is closed and only a handful of homes remain occupied. Even the churches stand silent and empty most of the year.

"The school is gone – torn down in 1980 – and the railway station went in 1979," Mason says. "The young people move out and there is no one to replace them. But," he adds, "it's a friendly place and I wouldn't want to live anywhere else."

Left: Moose was a welcome relief for the settlers' boring winter diet.

Below: A grain buyer snapped by Makinak photographer Anatole D'Aoust. In his scores of photos, D'Aoust left a record which portrays pioneer life representative not only of his community but also of all small settlements in the early 1900s.

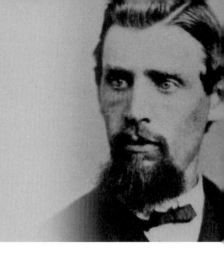

McArthur's Landing

Above, right: Peter McArthur.

ABOUT 1885 PIONEER LUMBERMAN PETER McARTHUR built a flat-bottomed sternwheel steamer called the *Saskatchewan* at the railway crossing in Westbourne and steamed her 3.2 km (2 miles) down the Whitemud River to his home. Thus was born the community which became known as McArthur's Landing, sometimes referred to as "The Landing." Linked by a spur line to the Manitoba and North Western Railway to the south and by water to massive Lake Manitoba, it grew into a thriving freight and supply centre.

"WE (CHILDREN) NEVER WEARIED OF LEANING ON THE RAILING BEHIND THE PADDLE WHEELS WATCHING THE RAINBOWS IN THE SPRAY."

McArthur built a fish plant and a lumber mill at the site to receive and process the fish and logs he brought in from Lake Manitoba and points north. The *Saskatchewan* was licensed to carry passengers and sometimes McArthur's family travelled with him. Years later his daughter, Agnes, wrote of those pleasant days aboard the sternwheeler: "We would back down the river a little way into Perch Creek to turn around. Then down the nine miles of the beautiful Whitemud, past Totogan, to the lake." She recalled how her mother would take her sewing machine along or play the little rosewood piano on board. "We (children) never wearied of leaning on the railing behind the paddle wheels watching the rainbows in the spray."

Peter McArthur had arrived in the Red River country in 1869 during the turbulent months that preceded the formal transfer of Rupert's Land and the North-West Territories from the Hudson's Bay Company to the Dominion of Canada. After a brief stint as bridge carpenter on the Dawson Route, a road then being constructed

to give access to Fort Garry (now Winnipeg), he answered the call for volunteers to protect government property against Métis leader Louis Riel.

The property in jeopardy was later described by McArthur as "…20 tons of pork and beans…stored in Dr. Schultz's warehouse." In later years McArthur was convinced that had these provisions been distributed as requested by the Metis when their buffalo hunt failed, the subsequent bitter confrontation at Red River would not have occurred.

Métis fears that their rights would be ignored in the impending transfer were aggravated by the unexplained activities of Dominion surveyors dragging measuring chains over the lands of established settlers. Then Ottawa fanned the smouldering embers by sending Governor McDougall to Red River before there was a formal transfer of title from the Hudson's Bay Company. Riel and his supporters forced the governor back across the border to Pembina. Then they seized Fort Garry, took control of the

controversial pork and beans, and on December 8, 1869, issued the Declaration of the People of Rupert's Land in which Riel created a provisional government.

In that same month Louis Riel took Peter McArthur and several others prisoner, among them Thomas Scott whom Riel later executed. McArthur escaped in January, was recaptured, and finally released in March. Then he went to Ottawa to appear before a parliamentary committee inquiring into the affairs of the Red River settlers.

In his memoirs, dictated shortly before his death in 1936, McArthur reveals his dissatisfaction with the conduct of various authorities involved in the dispute at Red River and expresses regret for his own role. "Time has deprived me of pride in our party's activities," he said, "and I have come to feel that all the Red River parties interested in the transfer of Rupert's Land, with the exception of the native tribes, made grave mistakes. The record of the local Indian bands was good and they had as much at stake in the transfer as anyone."

When the formal transfer was completed McArthur returned to Red River and made the first timber deal in the West for a stand of spruce on the Brokenhead River. He opened negotiations with the local Aboriginals by present-

ing a box of raisins to their chief. Before long he found himself agreeing to supply a plow and a grindstone, and for each family a sturgeon net, a dress length, and a quantity of beads. Recounting the transaction in his memoirs, McArthur dryly noted: "The chief thoughtfully provided me with the number of families."

He increased his timber interests over the years and built five steamboats, including the *Prince Rupert*, the first such vessel built within the province of Manitoba. His *Marquette* and *Northwest* plied the Assiniboine River as far west as Fort Ellice. In the remarkably high-water year of 1881 the *Marquette* navigated swollen waters as far as Fort Pelly.

The *Marquette's* collections book, written in neat hand and still in existence, reveals something of the commerce of the times. Cabin fare from Winnipeg to Grand Valley was $7, to Fort Ellice $12.50; meals were 50 cents. Freight lists for 1880-81 reveal an interesting variety of items which included an engine valve, lumber, shingles, windows, doors, and four kegs of nails. There was a buggy, bales of furs, a box of rabbits, a bundle of carpet, seven sacks of bacon and three wagons for Millford. Additional variety was provided by some tent poles, a box of eggs, twenty-nine hides, a bundle of sheepskins, four barrels of salt and five barrels of pork.

McArthur sold the *Marquette* and the *Northwest* in 1883 and embarked on a career as a manager of inland navigation for the Hudson's Bay Company. During this period he accomplished an incredible feat of engineering and navigation when he took three steamers and a barge from Winnipeg to Edmonton via Lake Winnipeg and the Saskatchewan River. Unfortunately, his high principles cost him his job with the company. A life-long prohibitionist, he refused to load a consignment of liquor for Edmonton. Dominion regulations of the time forbade liquor traffic in the North-West Territories and he incurred the wrath of the fur lords when he left the rum behind.

Never idle for long, McArthur turned his energies toward developing his northern lumber and fishing industries from The Landing. The Manitoba Gypsum Company located there, too, building a large wharf and warehouse for gypsum from their mines along Lake Manitoba. Farmers in the area with sons as young as ten hurried to the wharf at the blast of the steamboat whistle to help unload the 100 tons of gypsum regularly carried by the company boat. Barges brought in even more of the mineral and the extra cash helped many a farmer over the lean months until harvest.

The federal government operated a dredge to deepen the river and also ran boats to northern communities. Each year the government boat Henrietta embarked on a treaty money trip with a doctor, interpreter and Aboriginal agent. Flags flying, they called at each Aboriginal settlement along the lake to distribute blankets and stipends in accordance with treaties. Hudson's Bay Company boats sailed the same waters carrying supplies to the north and returning with bundles of furs.

As activities at McArthur's Landing increased, the cluster of dwellings grew to include a rooming house and hotel for the convenience of travellers and local bachelors. There was also a livery barn, store, and post office. In 1900 a school opened with an enrollment of twenty-five, but by then changing times were signalling the decline of the community.

The whistle of trains up the sides of Lake Manitoba in the first decade of the twentieth century replaced the whistle of steamboats and ended the era of riverboat traffic. Some of the buildings at The Landing were torn down and moved away; others eventually burned. Only the school outlived the settlement and served the surrounding district until 1954. For decades afterwards it stood at the roadside, the block letters of its name gradually fading into the weathered wood. Now, it too is gone.

Opposite: Peter McArthur built five steam ships, including the *Marquette*, to ply the rivers and lakes of pioneer Manitoba.

Below: Fort Garry in the early 1870s. When Riel and his Métis followers seized Fort Garry in 1869, they captured McArthur and several others and imprisoned them in the Fort. McArthur later felt that if the Métis had been treated fairly, the outbreak and the subsequent 1885 Riel Rebellion would not have occurred.

GHOST TOWNS OF MANITOBA • 50

MENNONITE VILLAGES

A UNIQUE SETTLEMENT PLAN was brought to Manitoba by the Mennonites in 1874. Each settlement contained four sections of land with a village huddled in the centre. Similar to the strategy of American settlers who camped with their covered wagons drawn into a circle for protection, the centralized villages had been adopted in Europe for the same reason.

Beginning with the founding of the sect in Switzerland in 1536, the Mennonite people had been persecuted – largely because of their Anabaptist and pacifist beliefs. Migrations to countries offering greater freedom became a way of life and in 1786 the Mennonites accepted Catherine the Great's invitation to move to Russia. Although she offered them freedom of religion and exemption from military service, she didn't tell them that the area they were about to settle was still partially inhabited by warring tribes of Turks and Tartars. When raids and massacres by these tribes became common, the sect established a system of villages, which were not only self-sufficient but also offered greater protection. Since this plan worked quite well, they brought it with them to Canada.

Villages consisted of up to thirty dwellings built close together and strung out on both sides of a wide road. The first homes were similar to those used by the Mennonites for two centuries before their departure from Russia. This pattern was a house-barn dwelling constructed of poles, mud, and sod, which sheltered family and livestock under one roof. The home, separated from the barn by a narrow corridor with doors at either end to keep out animal odours, was centrally heated by a large box-like brick heater, which could be used as oven, cookstove, and smokehouse.

Peter Barkman in the book, *Mennonite Memories*, describes his family's home in Manitoba: "Our first dwelling consisted of a sod house dug two feet into the ground, eighteen feet wide and forty-eight feet long. The walls of the building were made of thin tree trunks, having the interstices between the trunks filled with clay. The roof was likewise made of thin logs covered with mud.

Opposite: The village of Reinfeld in the late 1890s. It was typical of several dozen throughout southern Manitoba.

Left: Mennonites came to Manitoba because of the promise of religious toleration.

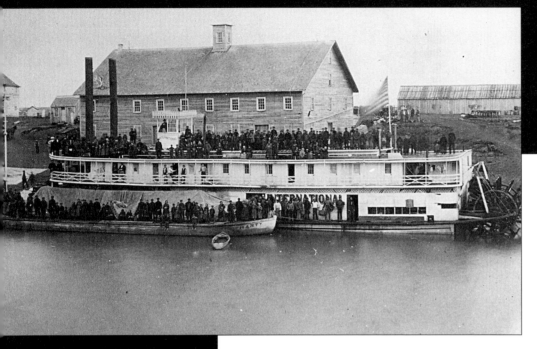

Thirty feet of the building was used as a dwelling and the remaining eighteen feet as a barn for the livestock."

Most families had flower and vegetable gardens close to their houses, with farmlands assigned so that each shared equally in both good and unproductive acreages. There was also a pasture, which was shared by everyone. Each village had a school which in the smaller settlements was also used as a church. The larger villages had a separate church building while almost every village had its own blacksmith shop and the larger ones often had mills and stores.

The villages also had their own system of government with elected officials. There was a "Schultz" (Mayor) and two assistants who acted as police, a "Hirtenschultz" (herdsman inspector), and a "Brandschultz" (fire inspector). Rounds were made every three weeks by these men to ensure that chimneys were kept clean and in safe condition.

In addition, there was a "Brand Aeltester" (chief fire inspector) who made an inspection every three years to see that everyone had a good ladder and a firehook sixteen feet long to pull pails of water from the wells. Failure to meet these requirements brought a reprimand and a warning that, should fire occur, the loss would not be compensated under their fire insurance scheme.

Each village had a school which in the smaller settlements was also used as a church.

The Mennonites also had their own mutual hail insurance plan as well as a "Waisenamt," a kind of credit union providing banking facilities. The people relied very little on non-Mennonites and even had their own midwives and bone setters for medical help. Some villages provided basic services for a number of other villages such as the flour mill at Blumenort and the wind-driven mills at Reinland and Rosenthal.

The villages were clustered in two areas of southern Manitoba on land set aside for them by the Canadian

Above: A typical Mennonite house-barn combination in 1955.

government. The east reserve, 36 km (25 miles) south of Winnipeg and east of the Red River, contained eight townships. The first group of about fifty families arrived in August 1874. It was with dismay that some of the newcomers viewed the barren looking land. The remoteness of the area – up to four days travel by oxen to Winnipeg – combined with the absence of any signs of civilization drove some of them to the United States.

When the second group arrived shortly after, one of its members, David Klassen, insisted that the Mennonites had been offered better land on the other side of the Red River and that he intended to investigate. His action caused a split.

Some settlers were satisfied to remain on the east reserve but the others followed Klassen to the west side of the Red River. This region became known as the west reserve. In time fifty-nine villages developed on the east reserve and seventy on the west, although only about forty-five on the east reserve were occupied and not all on the west reserve became functional. The

reason was that it soon became evident that the traditional village system, so useful in Russia, was not so easily adapted to Canada.

Government regulations required that each homestead be filed by an individual, although provision was made to permit the formation of farm villages with the land to be pooled. The modification, however, was not binding in law. If a settler was bankrupted or was even threatened with foreclosure, the village of which he was a part dissolved. Sometimes, to be nearer to his land, a farmer would move from the village to his own holding, even though such an action meant certain excommunication.

Then because rapid population increases caused a shortage of land, some young people moved north to establish their own homesteads. They, too, were shunned. Less strict branches of the sect emerged, however, and accepted the excommunicated, including people who later chose to live in new towns such as Rosenfeld, Altona and Gretna.

These towns appeared in 1882 when the Canadian Pacific Railway was extended south from Winnipeg through the eastern portion of the reserve. Similarly, with western extension of the railway along the north part of the reserve, Plum Coulee, Winkler, and Horndean were born. Such trading centres supplied more goods and better services than the old villages and the trend away from the traditional village system continued.

Commercial enterprises that had existed in the farm villages moved into the railway centres. The store at Neuanlage and the mill at Blumenort, for example, were moved to Gretna. Other businesses, like the store and mill at Reinland, simply folded. Even the large schools and churches transferred to the bigger centres with only the smallest remaining in the villages.

In the 1920s dissolution of the villages was speeded when the Provincial Department of Education began to enforce its regulations of compulsory school attendance.

Peter Dyck in his book, *The History of Haskett*, explains that the people of the village of Eichenfeld saw in the regulations an indirect threat to their religious doctrine of non-resistance. They decided to move out of the country. "An opening was found into Mexico," Dyck wrote, "and, beginning in 1923, trainload after trainload of emigrants left."

In addition to the village of Eichenfeld, emigration emptied other settlements – as did another development. Tractors and other machinery obviated the need for the intense co-operation that once had been necessary for survival. As the concept of individual farm holdings grew, more and more people moved from the villages, in many cases taking their buildings with them. The cumulative result was that most of the old villages became ghosts. By the early 1980s, though, a dozen or so typical Mennonite dwellings with the house and barn connected were still standing in Reinland – sturdy reminders of an era of simplicity and resourcefulness.

Below: Friedensfeld, 1955

METHVEN

FROM ITS BIRTH IN 1891 THE VILLAGE OF METHVEN, on the Canadian Pacific Railway about eight km (five miles) northwest of Wawanesa, seemed destined to be an important community. By 1900 businesses included lumber yards, livery stables, general stores and a hotel, among others. There were also two elevators – the Ogilvie Milling Company and the Lake of the Woods.

The Lake of the Woods used horses to operate the milling machinery, a motive power that had its problems. For instance, if the horses didn't walk fast enough the machinery slowed and plugged. This imminent problem was signalled to the operator by a change in the sound of the machinery. Thus alerted, he would rush in and shout colourful words of encouragement to the horses. Another problem was that the elevator was in a low-lying area. Water sometimes got into the storage pit and had to be pumped out by hand before grain was dumped. In later years a gas engine was installed but was reputed to be as balky as the horses.

In spite of difficulties, the elevators were busy places. In the mid-1890's one farmer, James McFadden, threshed 10,000 bushels of wheat and sold it for 90 cents a bushel. He put the money in a grain sack and took his fortune to the Merchant's Bank in Brandon. His timing was excellent as the price of grain dropped that afternoon.

But despite its elevators and variety of business places, Methven was destined for a short life. In the early 1900s most of its businesses closed or moved. The most commonly held theory was that its proximity to Wawanesa rendered Methven unnecessary. The goods and services needed by people in the area were insufficient to keep two towns flourishing.

Ironically, for decades the major landmark and link to the past was the problem-prone Lake of the Woods elevator. But it, too, became history when in 1967 the last two cars of grain were shipped. The nearly seventy-year-old structure was jacked up and, on sixty rubber tires, moved to the Hutterite Colony at Spring Valley. With the elevator gone, even the site of Methven was difficult to find. By the 1980s only a careful search might reveal, behind a tangle of scrub growth, parts of a wooden sidewalk, the remains of several buildings and a lonely front gate standing guard over a patch of nettles.

Left: A reminder of happier years in the remains of a basement.

MILLFORD

LOCATED AT THE FORK OF THE SOURIS RIVER AND OAK CREEK, Millford was born in 1879-80, flared briefly to prominence, then faded within a decade. It remains, however, one of Manitoba's best known ghost towns since it was the childhood home of author and feminist Nellie (Mooney) McClung. It lives in her book, *Clearing in the West*, and in other accounts passed along by Millford pioneers and their descendants.

One of the first settlers in the area was Nellie's older brother, Will Mooney. He came west from Ontario in the spring of 1879, fired by a friend's description of land where "a man could plow a furrow a mile long and never strike a stone and the feet of oxen are stained red with the juice of wild strawberries." While working with a survey crew, Will claimed land for himself, his father, and one brother, and spent the first winter cutting logs for a cabin. He lived in a tent with the sound of howling wolves for company and cold so intense it split trees wide open "and they cracked like pistol shots."

Will's parents, John and Letitia Mooney, joined him with the rest of the family in the summer of 1880. Nellie, only six at the time, later wrote of the fourteen-day journey from Winnipeg along the Portage and Yellowquill Trails: "We walked as much as we could, riding only when we got tired. I believe my mother walked the whole way for she liked to keep her eye on the whole procession."

The Mooneys had two oxcarts and a pony cart containing settlers' effects and one bed made up "in case of sickness." Because of the many mud holes, progress was slow and fellow travellers had to help one another along the trail. "Sometimes it took three yokes of oxen to draw a wagon out of a bad spot," wrote Nellie, "and even then the long grass beside the road had to be cut and thrown into the slippery, gummy mud to give the oxen a foot-hold."

It was near the end of September when the family left the main road and turned south toward the Assiniboine River. "The muddy roads with their terrors were past…The oxen, sensing the nearness of home, stepped livelier and everyone's spirits rose." They forded the river at dawn and reached the homestead 11 km (7 miles) distant at noon the same day.

"No one could fail to be thrilled with the pleasant spot Will found for us," Mrs. McClung commented in her book. "Away to the south, hazy in the distance stood the Tiger Hills; to the northwest the high shoulder of the

Opposite: Waddell and Brown's Store in 1882.

Above: Millford pioneers.

to subsisting on handouts from those who had taken their land.

Nevertheless, the Aboriginals' relationship with their new neighbours in the Millford area was friendly. Scottish settler Alex Reid, who wrote numerous letters to his family about life in the Canadian West, once described an amusing visit with Aboriginals camped near his farm: "I had quite a pow-wow with them. One of them would get his tom-tom and begin beating some tune…then jump up and down and dance around the fire like a turkey cock with all his feathers on his head; then I would jump up and follow him hee-hawing all the time. Jim Hill and I nearly killed them with laughing. He and I danced the Highland fling, he on one side of the fire and I on the other. The Indians rolled over and laughed to split their sides and said 'Nisishin' (good)."

Alex Reid had come from Scotland with his step-brother and settled in the Millford district in the spring of 1880. He saw the land fill up quickly with settlers from Ontario, England, Ireland, and Scotland. In November of that year he wrote, "…there is not a section of good land within a radius of fifteen miles of Millford vacant." Of the new village of Millford he noted: "…you can get provisions as cheap as Winnipeg plus the freight."

The founder of Millford was Major R.Z. Rogers from Grafton, Ontario, who travelled with Reid on the first steamboat up the Assiniboine River in the spring of 1880. The Major, "a man of considerable means," had acquired the land in 1879 on the advice of his brother-

Brandon Hills, dark blue and mysterious." Across the valley and along the creek banks, piles of buffalo bones gleamed whitely in the sun. The Mooneys later used them to edge their flower beds. Beginning in 1884, however, the bones became a source of income as settlers gathered them for fertilizer at five dollars a ton.

The thousands of tons of buffalo bones which covered the prairie told a tragic story. They were the consequence of a massive slaughter that in a few years had resulted in the death of virtually every animal in an original herd estimated at some 60 million. This slaughter also destroyed the Plains Aboriginals' proud way of life and forced them from independence

in-law, F.C. Caddy, who was a Dominion land surveyor. Caddy had surveyed Millford into 500 lots complete with public squares, a steamboat landing and, most important, a railway line which Rogers expected the CPR would run through the town.

In order to establish a milling industry and to provide homes for the workers and anyone else who could be persuaded to move West, Rogers hired a party of men who included Thomas Dewart, a carpenter from Norwood, Ontario. Construction began with the erection of a sawmill, a number of houses and, later, a gristmill. The town grew rapidly, although its 30 families weren't exactly the 500 envisioned by its promoters. In an article for the Glenboro Gazette, June 1945, W.A. Dewart, son of the original builder, listed businesses as follows: "Three hotels, three livery stables, two blacksmith shops, several general stores…Johnnie Wheeler's boot and shoe shop, where we got our long knee boots made; Doctors Butchard, White and Husband; photographers, lawyers, etc."

To the east of town stood the provincial registry office, a schoolhouse, and a church. Sadly, the first funeral in the church was that of the minister's three-year-old son. He died, wrote Nellie McClung, "…when the wild anemones were spreading their blue carpet over the prairie."

The town was also served by a post office with mail brought from Brandon on a more or less regular basis. Snow-blown trails and freezing temperatures, however, strained the endurance of even the most dedicated mail-driver, and the time and day of his weekly arrival became the subject of many wagers. According to Mrs. McClung, the old pessimist put his 25 cents each week against all takers that the mail wouldn't get through at all and twice during the winter of 1882 "raked in all the stakes."

Left: The community's most famous resident, popular author and women's rights champion Nellie McClung.

Below: Millford in the early 1880s.

Spring weather, too, presented problems. In 1882 the worst flood in years filled the lower level of the valley where Millford stood, swept away the Major's warehouse with 1,000 bags of flour and carried off the bridge over Oak Creek. Cellars were inundated and, for a time, the entire village was in danger of floating away. During the flood, the enterprising captain of a Souris River steamer attempted to follow one of the ravines that intersected the town and land freight at the back door of Hill and McLean's store. Major Rogers objected to this new service. He quite reasonably felt that a boat steaming up the street was a poor advertisement for his townsite.

The Major clung to the hope that Millford would attract new growth and industry, but his attempts to secure the necessary railway failed. Farmers, compelled to haul their grain nearly 50 km (30 miles) to Brandon, chafed at the delay. They also denounced the federal government's support of the CPR and its "monopoly clause" which prevented construction of any lines in a southerly direction from the CPR's main line. The clause was designed to protect the company from American competition. Unfortunately, it effectively eliminated provincial competition as well and left settlements entirely dependent upon the CPR.

COMPLAINTS NOTWITHSTANDING, THE RAILWAY TO MILLFORD FAILED TO MATERIALIZE IN TIME TO SAVE THE TOWN.

Complaints notwithstanding, the railway to Millford failed to materialize in time to save the town. When a branch line reached Glenboro in 1886, business was gradually diverted from Millford. One by one townspeople put their shops and homes on skids and moved them 25 km (16 miles) east to Glenboro or other towns on the rail line.

By this time, even the Major had abandoned his dreams and returned to eastern Canada. A few years later, when the railway finally passed through Millford at the location he had designated, there was little left of his town but piles of rubble, empty cellars, and a few lonely graves on the hillside.

A cairn was erected in 1945 to mark the site of Millford. It was inscribed with a tribute by Nellie McClung to those who "…travelled hopefully in spite of everything. They had something that kept them from despair when the crops failed, the cow died, the payment on the binder was due, the children were sick and the nearest doctor was eighty miles away. They trusted in God and went on triumphantly…"

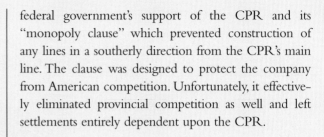

Above: A cairn erected in 1945 bears a tribute by Nellie McClung.

Below: An abandoned business, typical of many, once common in rural Manitoba.

MOORE PARK

MOORE PARK, NEAR THE JUNCTION OF PROVINCIAL ROADS 468 AND 353, 28 km (16 miles) south of Minnedosa, began life as Dooley. But when the CPR came through in 1904, it was renamed Moore Park in honour of Colonel W.P. Moore who owned land on which the townsite was located. He donated five acres of land for a park.

Moore Park was typical of many prairie towns. During its boom years it had flourishing businesses, schools, churches, lodges and other services, including a three-storey boarding house owned by Colonel Moore. While the community wasn't destined to survive, it was to be warmly remembered by many who lived there in an era when life was more placid and general stores sold almost everything a family might ever need.

In George Harland's book, *They Called It Odanah*, he recalls shopping in Moore Park, with particularly strong recollections of medicines then available for the pioneers: "…some people believed a few drops of coal oil on a spoonful of sugar was a good way to relieve a sore throat. A more popular cure-all, however, was Dr. Thomas' Eclectic Oil. This could be purchased at any drug store and was found in most homes. It was alleged to cure sore throats, earache, sprains and bruises and many other ailments."

In those days before laws against misleading advertising there was no reason to be sick — at least according to manufacturers of patent medicine. If Dr. Thomas' Eclectic Oil didn't prove efficacious, then there were products such as Carter's Little Liver Pills, Gin Pills for the Kidneys, Dr. Chase's Nerve Food or Lydia Pinkham's Pills for Pale People.

In those horse and buggy days people who didn't have access to or, more likely, money for patent medicines could choose from a vast array of do-it-yourself home cures. For instance, a cake of yeast soaked overnight in tepid water with a bit of sugar produced a liquid claimed to have restorative powers. Wild herbs and bark made into tea cured stomach upsets and even flu, while cuts and sores were often treated with

Left: Moore Park Cemetery, reminder of a once thriving community. Moore Park was originally spelled as one word, but in 1971 was officially changed to the two word form.

Above: Moore Park school vans 1912. Getting to school was an adventure then, but school consolidation later helped spell the end of the town.

Below: Working the land in 1910.

concerts and a variety of sports and parades – especially the splendour of the Orangemen's parade.

Every July 12 the Minnedosa Lodge and the Moore Park Orange Lodge provided a spectacle for the townspeople. William of Orange, represented by a brightly attired lodge member mounted on a white horse, was followed by a fife and drum band, officials in regalia and the rank and file. Afterwards there would be a dance at the Lodge Hall since Moore Park residents, like those of other frontier communities throughout the newly settled land, loved dancing.

While Moore Park was typical of many prairie towns in its social activities, it was also typical in its demise. An expected postwar boom following the First World War did not materialize. The town nevertheless remained fairly stable until after the Second World War, when it enjoyed an increase in population. The surge proved only temporary. By 1958 farm economy was in a slump and many farmers left, resulting in severe loss of trade for the town's businesses.

Balm of Gilead made by cooking the buds of black-poplar trees. For the more adventurous – or perhaps desperate – skunk oil was thought to be a sure cure for arthritis, rheumatism, and similar afflictions. A minor shortcoming was preparing the medicine. After catching the skunk, it had to be skinned, cleaned and roasted slowly for it was the fat that was used. Was it effective? Well, what disease – or person – would dare linger in such an aromatic household, rheumatism or not?

Whether people survived because of the various treatments or in spite of them is debatable. But the people of Moore Park were evidently a healthy and vibrant lot. They worked hard and enjoyed community suppers,

School and church consolidation, as well as increasingly better roads to larger centres, had a negative effect. In the 1980s, Frank Hunter, one of the last residents, recalled: "The town lost all its businesses because of the big stores in Brandon and Minnedosa."

THIS USED TO BE A THRIVING TOWN… ALL THAT'S LEFT HERE NOW IS THE COMMUNITY HALL AND THERE'S BEEN SOME TALK OF CLOSING IT.

Even the park didn't survive. Hunter related, "After a while the fence came down and when they took the railway up in 1979 they piled the ties in there. Most of them are gone now. They were sold for fence posts, some of them trucked as far away as Denver. It doesn't look much like a park now.

"This used to be a thriving town…All that's left here now is the Community Hall and there's been some talk of closing it. Some people still live here though and work in Brandon and the rest are mostly retired. There's just a few of us left in Moore Park."

In his Valley Vistas column in the *Brandon Sun,* December 30, 1972, Dr. Peter Lorenze Neufeld wrote what could be called Moore Park's obituary: "I find it very difficult to see why our federal government permits closing post offices while it simultaneously supports costly rural route mail services out of larger towns, permits abandonment of rail branch lines, why small village churches couldn't be served by lay and student ministers, why we allow closing of elementary schools in villages…an ideal country has a logical balance of cities, towns, villages, farms. Especially the trend in Manitoba with over half our people concentrated in Winnipeg frightens me.

"Nothing makes me sadder than to watch a thriving rural community die."

Above: Manitoba farms in the early 1900s. In the following years when machinery began to replace oxen and horses, fewer men were required. Farms were consolidated and improved roads meant that larger centres became supply points. Many small communities then began their journey into oblivion.

MOUNTAIN ROAD

WHEN UKRAINIAN SETTLERS FIRST CAME to the isolated area called Mountain Road, near the Riding Mountains, they could not have imagined they would build a magnificent cathedral here. That this unlikely dream took root in their hearts and became a reality, is a tribute to their deep faith, and to the courage and gratitude with which they met the difficulties of life.

Certainly, the difficulties were many. Eli Zahodniak and his family, who arrived in 1896, gave generous assistance to those who followed but the sheer numbers of immigrants meant hardship for many. Eleven families arrived in 1898 and another fifteen in 1899. Finding good farmland still open to homesteading was a challenge for them but for the 104 people who came in 1903, it was almost impossible. Many had to use their meagre resources to buy land from the railway or the government. This meant that four families often had to make do on only a quarter section.

At first settlers shared the homes or shanties built by others before them. Some even slept in cow pens or makeshift barns. The men walked more than 33 km (21 miles) to Neepawa to look for work and once there slept outdoors for a few days, surviving on dry bread and water. If there were no jobs, they walked home again.

When they arrived in the country, many did not have the kind of clothing needed for Canada's harsh winters. Even with the help of others, there was not enough warm clothing to go around. In spite of the cold, however – or perhaps because of it – the men worked hard cutting wood in the Riding Mountains, often with only a hand axe, to sell to other settlers and in the towns for 25 cents a cord.

Women and children helped clear the land for planting, a little each year. When they managed to produce a few rows of potatoes, life looked good. Once they established a flock of chickens and acquired a cow, it improved dramatically. In addition to better food for their families, they now had cream to sell or trade along with cheese, butter, and eggs.

They built their homes of logs, chinked with straw and manure, plastered with mud and whitewashed with

Opposite: 1890: Immigrants arriving in Manitoba on CPR train.

Left: Silent and empty now, this abandoned home once sheltered a Mountain Road family.

lime. Usually, the roof was of sod or thatch but occasionally shiplapped with wood from the lumber mill. At first the houses consisted of only a single room with an earthen floor, but each provided shelter, even comfort, for families of up to ten or more. Mattresses filled with hay served as beds. Furniture was simple and handmade.

Their ancient faith was the mainstay of the settlers' lives. So much so, that it was not unusual in the early days for them to walk the eight km (five miles) to Hun's Valley each Sunday to attend Mass at St. Elizabeth of Hungary church. There, too, they celebrated weddings and funerals and enjoyed the pleasure of visiting with neighbours who spoke a language similar to their own. Nevertheless, in 1904 they formed a committee to build a log church at Mountain Road, where they could worship in the familiar Ukrainian Catholic liturgy of their homeland.

Their children went to be educated in the first school built in the community about 1907. At the peak of Mountain Road's population there were two schools with 94 children enrolled. When they were considered old enough, perhaps 14, many of them left school to work at other farms or at jobs in the towns. Any wages earned went to help their struggling families. Because of their youth, homesickness was a problem as was their rudimentary grasp of English.

Cindy (Kolesar) Williams, remembers her grandmother Safroniuk relating a story of a misunderstanding over language that happened while she worked for a family in another town. When her employer directed her to put the cream away in the crock, the English words confused the youngster who thought she said to throw the cream into the bush.

"So, of course, my Babka wouldn't do it," Williams explained. "The woman became angry and repeated her request. Still Babka refused. But at last she gave in and threw the cream in the bush!"

The young people who worked away from home, sometimes had to walk distances of up to 50 km (30 miles) to visit their families on the weekends. Still, they summoned the energy to sing and dance with friends after church or play musical instruments for hours at a time.

At first, they gathered in barns, implement sheds or the school, where they also organized concerts for the community. But social prospects improved when, during the thirties, Matty Baranuik donated land for a hall. Parishioners, with Eli Kostenchuk as foreman, pitched in to build it. As always, the women contributed their efforts, cooking wonderful meals and helping out with whatever events took place.

Although the village of Mountain Road never grew very large, one source notes there was a restaurant and shoemaker shop in the community. Four stores also operated in the village, one at each corner of the crossroads. Mike Zollen, Mike Yakiwchuk, Matt Baranuik, and Victor Rudko were the four owners. Eli Kostenchuk took over one of the stores in 1953 operating it along with the post office for 30 years, long after the others had gone. Williams has fond childhood memories of this store, "Babka would give us a dime and we'd run over to pick up the mail and buy Pink Elephant popcorn."

BECAUSE OF
THEIR YOUTH,
HOMESICKNESS
WAS A PROBLEM
AS WAS THEIR
RUDIMENTARY
GRASP OF
ENGLISH.

Below: A typical Ukrainian home.

Her grandmother's patience extended in many directions, from teaching her grandchildren to paint Easter eggs to putting up with their childish hi-jinks. One bit of mischief involved the church bell, which hung in a tower next to the church. It was only to be rung at Easter except to announce someone's death but the game was to ring it anyway and see if you could run home before it stopped. One day, when she was alone picking berries in a field between the church and her grandparents' house, Cindy decided to give it a try.

"There I was ringing away and all afternoon Babka kept getting phone calls asking who had passed away! I really got heck for that."

The Great Depression of the 1930s brought a return to hard times for the Mountain Road area. Dry spells, rust, and low prices for grain and livestock combined to force more than one farm to the brink of bankruptcy and some families left to look for greener pastures.

Even very young children did what they could to help the family coffers. According to W. Smith in *Rosedale Remembers 1884-1984* (published by the Municipality of Rosedale), the kids cashed in when the municipality offered a bounty of five cents for a pair of crow's feet, and three cents for a gopher tail. "If the gopher's tail was extra long," Smith wrote, "they would cut it in two for twice the payment."

Water was scarce during those years except at Polonia where people from neighboring towns were welcome to collect water at one or another of the good springs in the valley. In fact the people were so grateful for the water that the Mountain Road priest went to bless its location.

Among the dedicated priests who served at Mountain Road one stands out more than most. This was the architect priest, Reverend Philip Ruh, O.M.I. who came to Canada in 1911 to look after the spiritual needs of Ukrainian immigrants. He built a monastery and an orphanage, as well as churches in many locations in the country: Leduc and High River in Alberta; St. Catherines and Kenora in Ontario, Cooks Creek and Portage la Prairie in Manitoba, and one in Chicago, Illinois. So it was as a priest thoroughly familiar with the art of creating beautiful buildings, that Father Ruh came to the parishioners of Mountain Road in 1924.

Here he found a devout people badly in need of a larger church, and he immediately set out to help them achieve it. What they accomplished together exceeded even their most cherished hopes.

Each parishioner pledged 50 days of free labour as well as some cash or livestock to be auctioned or sold. Volunteers under the direction of Father Ruh and one hired carpenter began by preparing a concrete foundation. After that, everything was built of wood, cut, milled and hauled from the Riding Mountains, planed, shaped and lifted into place by hundreds of willing hands.

Schoolchildren, too, got into the act. Jessie Safroniuk, a schoolgirl at Mountain Road when the church was being built, told her granddaughters how at recess, the teacher would give them handfuls of bent nails along with hammers to straighten them out. The nails then were used in the construction.

In the end, St. Mary's Ukrainian Catholic church, built in the shape of a cross, measured 120 feet long, 100 feet wide, and 128 feet in height to the top of the cross on the dome. This 'wooden cathedral', as it came to be known, was supported by more than 40 pillars and boasted no less than 17 doors.

The basic building was completed in 1925 at a cost of approximately $18,000. This was an incredible feat, considering that it was valued by Montreal architects of the time at $175,000. There were no pews at first and no electric lights. But there was room for a thousand people to stand or kneel and lamps and candles sufficed for light until electricity was installed.

A chapter in Rosedale Remembers includes this lovely view of the church, "On a winter night with lights from 300 electric lamps streaming across the snow through 130 stained glass windows, it was a fabulous sight."

Each year improvements were made, tile on the floor, paintings on the ceiling and walls, a thousand decorative touches, statues, and stained glass. The women sewed altar cloths embroidered in traditional Ukrainian motifs and made artificial flowers. They attended to the cleaning of the church, laundering the linens and keeping everything in beautiful condition.

The fame of the church grew, drawing thousands of visitors every year from across Canada and the United States, Iceland, Norway, South Africa, England and Scotland. The parish worshipped there for forty-one years. Then tragedy struck.

On August 19, 1966, Jim Kolesar was standing in a doorway across the road from the church, looking out at the rain, when he witnessed a lightning bolt hit the building and set it aflame.

"Shingles flew everywhere," he says, "And the smoke started coming up; I knew it was done for. There was nothing we could do except alert the neighbours and someone phoned for help."

Unfortunately, in spite of all efforts to halt the blaze – parishioners with buckets of water, fire trucks from Erickson and a nearby Hutterite Colony with hoses and water tanks -- the water soon ran out and St. Mary's Church burned to the ground.

Bystanders wept for the 'wooden cathedral' they or their fathers had built with their own hands. But they were not defeated. Statues and other religious symbols had been carried from the church before it collapsed and some of these were restored for use in a new, smaller church built on the same site the following year.

Today, in a new millenium, the hamlet of Mountain Road has all but disappeared. Besides St. Mary's Ukrainian Catholic Church, only a house, a community hall and a few abandoned buildings mark its location. But a priest from Minnedosa still comes twice a month to the church to celebrate the age-old liturgies and supply spiritual nourishment to a faithful community.

Above: The arrival of the Countess of Dufferin heralded a new era of immigration.

MOWBRAY

A 1980 VISIT WITH ARCHIE AND LILLIE SCOTT AT their farm near the ghost town of Mowbray was like stepping into the past. The sprawling farmland that had been home to eighty-year-old Lillie and her brother, Archie, for fifty years was not only part of the section on which the village of Mowbray was built but also framed a view that had scarcely changed in a century. "Look!" said Archie, pointing north toward a breathtaking panorama of hills and forest. "You can see clean across to the other side of the Pembina Valley."

Before the Scott family moved to this site in 1930, they farmed nearby and retained vivid memories of a time and way of life that has passed into history.

"My father, Henry Scott, was the first man to take up land in this area between the Pembina hills and the International Border," Lillie explained. "He came out from Simcoe, Ontario, in the late 1870s with his father and brother. My grandfather, I believe, filed on a quarter section near Morden and my father came on here. That was before Morden existed, just Nelsonville.

"He stopped with Mennonite families along the way, carried only a fry pan, a big knife, some flour, and a piece of sowbelly (pork). He came to the top of Valley Hill and saw nothing but prairie. Then he took his butcher knife and cut sod and brush for a shelter. Later he walked south until he came to the boundary line."

Here Scott found what he was looking for – land with plenty of water and wood. "Wood was in great demand south of the border, my father knew he could sell it. He settled on a half section for himself and one for his brother, George. Later he went to Saskatchewan and gave the Manitoba land to his father. But at the time of the Riel Rebellion (1885) he had to high-tail it back here with the Métis chasing him part of the way. Eventually he settled on the half section a mile west of here."

The farm where Archie and Lillie Scott lived at the time of our visit, had been home-steaded by Andrew Johnston exactly one hundred years before, and the

Centre: This abandoned building is a link to livelier times when Mowbray residents enjoyed dances, concerts, socials and oyster suppers.

Above: A store at Mowbray with no customers.

Below: Brother and sister Archie and Lillie Scott lived on the same section of land as Mowbray for over 50 years.

three-room log house where he lived with his wife and six children still stood in the pasture behind the Scott home. In 1884 the house became the first post office in the area. Postal service was continued by the Johnstons for more than twenty years, with Mrs. Johnston succeeding her husband as postmaster after his death in 1897. Archie Scott recalled that the mail wagon was driven into the nearby log barn.

According to Lillie Scott, the Johnstons' little home not only accommodated the post office business and the large Johnston family, but was used as a stopping place for travellers, too: "I used to wonder if they slept in two tiers down there!"

When it became known that the Canadian Pacific Railway would be extended southeast from Snowflake into the Mowbray district, location for a townsite became a much debated issue. "They had an awful time deciding where it would be," Lillie remarked. However, the availability of a good water supply was the deciding factor and the creek running through Johnston land the final choice.

A general store was built at the site by Alf Garrett in time for the arrival of the railway in 1902. Soon there were two elevators, a railway station, livery barn, and a blacksmith shop with a poolroom and barbershop at the back and a dance hall above. There was also a lumberyard, machine shed, flour house, coal storage shed, and a dozen or so homes.

There was even a jail, although it was apparently used only once. The distinction went to an enterprising Metis. According to local residents, his felony occurred during the days when bounty was paid on wolves with the hide, complete with ears, proof of claim. This Metis presented his hide, ears intact, to the town clerk who cut the ears off and paid the bounty. The Metis kept the hide and

fashioned realistic artificial ears, which he sewed on. The number of times he presented the same hide with its new ears is not recorded. The clerk, however, discovered the hoax and had the Metis arrested.

Of greater concern to residents than a false-eared wolf hide was fire. It was a constant threat to Mowbray's wood buildings. In 1908 the livery barn and blacksmith's shop burned, as did one of the elevators and the first railway station. The last two were rebuilt, although the elevator was again destroyed by fire in 1931.

In the early years of the village the post office was moved from the Johnston farm to the general store in Mowbray. This store became a social centre with lively checker and whist tournaments in the back room. For other entertainment there were garden parties on the CPR lawn, box and pie socials, baseball games, tennis, and even "riding to the hounds," although it bore only passing resemblance to the English sport.

"We had a bunch of hounds," Miss Scott told us, "so did Robbie Johnston. That would be just about the time the town was settled. The men all went together on horseback, out in January in the cold, chasing around after wolves and coyotes. They would choose up sides and whoever lost had to pay for an oyster supper.

"Later there were dances and concerts. There was a lot of talent, a lot of fun, more than people have nowadays." Lillie recalled travelling to these affairs in a grain box on a sleigh: "The roads would be built way up with snow and if you ever got off you were in trouble." Dances were held in private homes as well as in the Mowbray Hotel, and many concerts presented in the second storey of the local school.

As was often the case during western settlement, a school district was formed several years before the village existed. In 1884 Mowbray School was built about 1.5 km (1 mile) northeast of the present townsite. This school was replaced in 1906 by two new schools. One of these, a further 1.5 km (1 mile) northeast, retained the name Mowbray; the other, in the village of Mowbray, was called Boundary School in recognition of the

International Boundary within a few yards of the schoolhouse door.

Part of the charm of schooldays at Mowbray was the proximity of the boundary line and the opportunity for village students to mix with their American counterparts. Until the late 1920s children from North Dakota attended classes in Boundary School, some living close enough to stroll across the road at noon for lunch in the United States. Teachers sometimes boarded at American homes and the school's water supply was hauled daily from a well on the American side.

Stuart and Muriel Johnston's history of Mowbray, *Lest We Forget*, describes travel between the two countries as "quite lenient." Doctors went wherever they were needed on either side, neighbours visited freely back and forth, farm goods were sold, and Mowbray housewives shopped for bargains in American stores.

Travellers from the U.S. often stayed at the Mowbray Hotel while they waited for or disembarked from a train. When prohibition came to North Dakota in 1919 the hotel's liquor business soared. In fact until local option stopped the sale of beverages in Mowbray, the hotel existed mainly on American trade. The Johnstons wrote: "Weekends during the summer there were often as many as fifty Americans who parked their cars on what was called 'Rum Row' just across the border from the school, while they walked over to the hotel to quench their thirst."

But both prosperity and informality were ending. Boundary patrols, established during the 1930s to pre-vent smuggling and illegal trade, also reduced casual traffic over the border. Then in 1935 railway service to Mowbray was cut to one train a week. Coupled with the effects of the world-wide depression, local drought and plagues of grasshoppers, it was a near mortal blow for the village. The end came when World War Two drained young men from the village. When they returned most settled elsewhere.

Rural life changed even more with the trend to larger farms and owners who lived up to 80 km (50 miles) away. To Lillie Scott, it was not a change for the better. "The valley used to be thickly populated," she said wistfully. "But most of the people are gone. Our nearest neighbour is two miles away. There is no one in Mowbray now except our two nephews, Richard and Larry, who work our farm.

"We are trying to keep the land until they can take over. We won't sell, there would be no possibility of getting it back. If only we could have what we used to have – our own chickens and meat and garden. Clothing was a problem, money was a problem but we had our own fuel, our own food.

"You felt so very free...you felt so good all the time. I am very thankful I had that experience."

Left: A time and a way of life passed into history. Mowbray today is little more than a field.

Above: The CPR station at Mowbray survived as a house.

"WEEKENDS DURING THE SUMMER THERE WERE OFTEN AS MANY AS FIFTY AMERICANS WHO PARKED THEIR CARS ON WHAT WAS CALLED 'RUM ROW' JUST ACROSS THE BORDER FROM THE SCHOOL..."

NEELIN

THE GHOST TOWN OF NEELIN, tucked in a fold of hills between Rock Lake and Lake Louise in the Pembina River Valley, is more like a park than a deserted village. Although its population dwindled to about a dozen by 1980, Neelin's lawns and gardens – even its vacant lots – were kept neatly groomed.

The Pembina River runs nearby as does Badger Creek, a waterway that once was the scene of a bogus gold rush. Old-timers say that during the 1930s the creek was staked for a distance of 18 km (11 miles) from Neelin to Cartwright after a swimmer claimed to have found a gold nugget in the creek bed.

"It was just a joke," an early resident explained. "But word spread all over the country." Although no gold ever was found, the joke lived on in gold-painted nuggets that passed from pocket to pocket for years afterwards.

Long before the lure of gold, however, rumours of a railway and tales of rich farmland enticed homesteaders to the Neelin Valley. Among the early settlers was Joseph Neelin, upon whose land the townsite of Neelin was later located. Neelin came to the district from Winnipeg in 1881 after suffering overwhelming personal and financial losses in the city. The victim of a land swindle, his young daughter dead of smallpox, he came to the valley with his family in search of a new beginning.

In 1896 he completed the two-storey family home that still stands just outside the western limits of the village. Built of prairie granite picked in the hills and plastered with lime burned in a nearby kiln, its sturdy walls have sheltered succeeding generations. Neelin's granddaughter, Frances Gillies, her husband and family lived there for many years.

Flowers bloomed against the walls of the old house and throughout the wide grounds, enhancing the park-like aspect of the village. In the farmyard a spring ran as clear and cold as it did when Joseph Neelin chose the homesite. The family believe that in earlier days the site was an Aboriginal camping place since arrowheads, stone hammers, and other artifacts have been found nearby.

Frances Gillies' father, Frank Neelin, who was born in the district in 1889, remembered as a boy watching

Centre: To reduce damage to grain crops, for years Manitoba paid a bounty for gopher tails. In 1919 a government pamphlet bragged that in one week school children killed 150,000 gophers.

Opposite: Early settlers took advantage of nearby frozen rivers and creeks to cut the ice for the preservation of food. The blocks of ice were often packed in sawdust and stored for use year round.

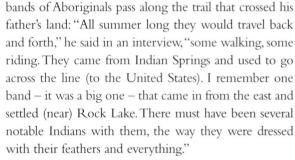

bands of Aboriginals pass along the trail that crossed his father's land: "All summer long they would travel back and forth," he said in an interview, "some walking, some riding. They came from Indian Springs and used to go across the line (to the United States). I remember one band – it was a big one – that came in from the east and settled (near) Rock Lake. There must have been several notable Indians with them, the way they were dressed with their feathers and everything."

But the nomadic life of the Aboriginals drew to a close as more and more white settlers came to the Neelin area following the government land survey of 1879. "In a very few years there were people on every half-section if not quarter-section," Frank Neelin said. "When I was going to school there were two or three times as many people as there is now."

Few services were available in the early years. Farmers took their grist as far as Emerson, 160 km (100 miles) away, until a local mill was built in 1883. The first

of a dozen or so lime kilns were built about that time, too, as there was an abundance of limestone in the area and plenty of wood for firing.

According to Frank Neelin the construction of these primitive-looking kilns required great skill. "It took an expert to build the firebox of prairie granite

"WHEN I WAS GOING TO SCHOOL THERE WERE TWO OR THREE TIMES AS MANY PEOPLE AS THERE IS NOW."

stones that would take four-foot logs and be strong enough to hold tons of limestone above it," he explained. "It took several days, maybe a week, of steady firing to burn the stone."

The remains of one of the kilns lie in the woods not far from the site of an elegant home built before the turn of the century by pioneer Robert Bernard Watson. Watson, a man of "aristocratic manner and bearing,"

built the house on a knoll overlooking Lake Louise, one of the finest views in the district.

Sadly, the house has long since been abandoned and the stone and stucco walls have tumbled beyond repair. An observation gallery that Watson built on the second floor tilts crazily skyward, the pastel-coloured stucco is crumbling to dust, and stone steps that once led to a beautiful sunken garden now go nowhere.

But Watson is remembered for more than his distinctive home. He was one of the district's earliest settlers and one of those credited with building and operating its first grist and sawmill. It wasn't until 1905, however, that the first train whistle echoed in the valley. It was a branch line of the Canadian Northern Railway, built through the area south and west from Greenway to Adelpha near Wakopa.

"It was known as the Wakopa line," laughed Frances Gillies. "But the engine always had trouble getting out of the valley so they called it the Wakopush!"

Trains were soon running three times a week from Greenway and back again on alternate days. Harry Bolton and George Way came from Cartwright in 1905 to open Neelin's first general store and the Western Grain Company built an elevator the same year. Other businesses followed, including a post office, hardware store, blacksmith, boarding house and a second elevator. By 1910 the village had a private bank operated by J. Laughlin which was later taken over by the Bank of Toronto. Later still the building served as the town high school and then as an Anglican church.

Bill Henwood, whose parents ran the Neelin boarding house, recalled that the village also had a restaurant, lumberyard, curling rink, and an open-air skating rink, which drew such crowds "that if you wanted to get on you had to be there by seven o'clock. And the schoolhouse dances! It was horses in those days, of course, and if you weren't there by

Above, left: Joseph Neelin's home, built in 1896 of prairie granite and plaster.

Above: Remains of a lime kiln in the Neelin area where pioneers produced their own plaster.

eight o'clock you couldn't get your horse in the barn."

Neelin's first school was Roseberry, built in the mid 1880s about three km (two miles) northeast of the village site. According to an article in the Southern Manitoba Review, the school was moved to the village in 1909 by farmers using twenty teams of horses. The same article notes that one of the early teachers was fired because of his foreign accent. Another, with extraordinary stamina, pedalled his bicycle each Friday afternoon to his home in Grandview some 225 km (135 miles) and "back again for school on Monday morning."

While the bicycle ride over dirt country roads was undoubtedly a challenge, many teachers probably would have preferred it to another that for many years confronted them in summer on Monday mornings – counting gopher tails. In an attempt to reduce gopher damage in the grain fields, the Manitoba government sponsored an annual contest that called on school children to "wage war on small pests as only boys and girls can do."

A 1919 pamphlet issued to schools bragged that in 1917, 150,000 gophers had been caught by Manitoba school children in one week alone. "Boys and girls are specially fitted and inclined to do a great work in our Province," the pamphlet stated. Teachers were instructed to tally the tails and enter the appropriate credit beside each child's name, after which the gopher tails were to be burned. The pamphlet even suggested the proper method: "This can be easily done on a little fire in the schoolyard in celebration of the saving to the Province."

For each gopher tail the children received a bounty of 2 1/2 cents and the assurance that this was only part of the reward: "For surely," the provincial pamphlet read, "dead gophers are worth as much to your father as to the government."

Frances (Neelin) Gillies, who attended school at Neelin during the 1930s, remembers taking part in numerous gopher hunts. "They would be so thick in the fields," she recalled, "we would run with our syrup pails full of water, empty them down a hole in the ground, and wait for the gopher....We put the tails in a matchbox, all lined up like wooden matches, and sprinkled them with salt to preserve them."

By this time, however, the bounty had dropped: "We got a penny a piece for them," Mrs. Gillies said. "And to us that was a lot of money."

It was a reflection of the times. Years of depression and widespread drought had affected all areas of life and strained the resources of the province. Even the relative prosperity of World War Two did not entirely restore the economy or save from extinction a number of Manitoba towns. Neelin was among them.

"It took only about four years after the war for Neelin to go down," Bill Henwood recalled. The village could not compete with larger centres like Cartwright and Killarney, which were becoming more accessible as roads improved and the motor vehicle came into common use. In addition, the number of people in the district decreased as modern machinery replaced the horse and brought about a trend toward larger farms.

In 1961 the railway lifted the track west of Neelin, ending the era of the old "Wakopush" line. For years afterwards one train a week came from the east as far as Neelin but in 1978 it, too, was discontinued and with it the services of the town's two elevators.

Meanwhile, Neelin had lost its school to consolidation and its churches to larger congregations in other towns. In 1967 the last store closed and by the eighties, except for a handful of homes, Neelin was history. But village pride remains intact; the United church is kept in repair and in 1995 a centennial reunion attracted over 300 former residents and friends to the village. Today, seven or eight families still call Neelin home.

Above: The ruins of pioneer Robert Bernard Watson's elegant dream home.

NELSONVILLE

NELSONVILLE WAS THE LARGEST TOWN IN MANITOBA to flourish, then disappear. Its history began in the spring of 1877 when Adam Nelson Sr. settled some 130 km (78 miles) southwest of Winnipeg. He had purchased a section of land before coming west with his wife, six sons and one daughter, intending to farm. On arriving, however, they discovered the folly of purchasing land without first seeing it – their farm, instead of being open prairie, was covered with trees.

Nelson was undaunted. He saw the need for sawmills and gristmills and decided to turn his bad judgement into a profit. When some property on nearby Silver Creek was offered to him he returned to Ontario and purchased equipment necessary for establishing the mills.

An unusually mild fall and winter in 1877-78 allowed the mill machinery to be brought up the Red River to Emerson in November 1877. It also enabled the Nelsons to complete their new home before Christmas. It was a large building with a thatched roof, a comfortable contrast to the shacks and worn-out tent, which had provided their temporary shelter.

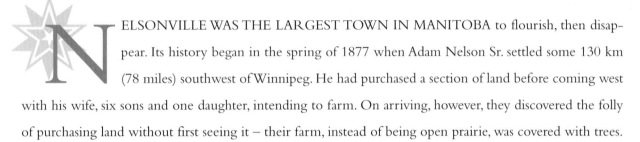

With lumber available, settlement intensified in the surrounding area and the community of Nelsonville was born. Within three years there were a variety of businesses including three general stores, two hotels, three law offices, two large livery and feed barns and a week-

ly newspaper called the *Mountaineer*. In addition, numerous residences – all nicely landscaped – gave the town an assuring air of permanency.

By 1882, when Nelsonville incorporated into the town of Nelson and a town hall was built, a land boom in Winnipeg thrust land prices in that city from $100 to upwards of $1,000 a foot. Although Nelson was 130 km (78 miles) from the provincial capital, purchasers, seized by the same frenzy, paid entrepreneurs up to $1,000 a lot in the embryo town.

Even though rapid growth swelled the population to more than 1,000, no railway materialized. Farmers had to haul their grain to Emerson, for some an arduous journey of over 112 km (70 miles). But this long trek proved an asset to a colourful citizen called Billy Brown. He erected a stopping house mid-way between Mountain City and Emerson, little troubled by the fact that he didn't own the land. He had squatted on

Centre: Pre-fab homes like this one often provided later immigrants with their first "little house on the prairie."

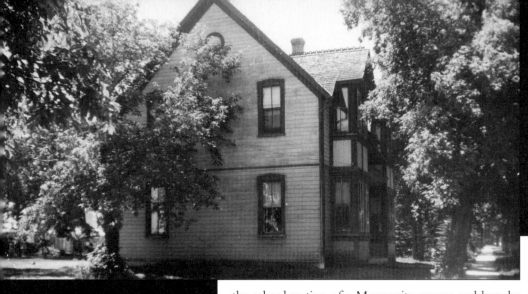

Above: Remnant of a once bustling community.

IN 1883 THE CPR'S PEMBINA BRANCH LINE WAS BUILT AND MISSED NELSON BY 12.5 KM (8 MILES).

the school section of a Mennonite reserve and here he served the men on their journeys to and from Emerson.

A jolly, personable man with luxuriant white hair and beard, a short, rotund build and a habit of wearing high boots and a red vest, he looked like a transplanted Santa Claus. In fact, old-timers reported that the resemblance was startling. To the surrounding Mennonites, however, Billy wasn't Old St. Nick. He was a devil.

The fact that his Halfway House had a liquor license was distressing to the Mennonites who lived a strict life and shunned alcohol. It was, by contrast, regarded as a boon by many thirsty visitors who enjoyed their host even though some suspected that the "champagne" he sold for $5 a quart was nothing more than gooseberry wine.

Another colourful character of the time was Tom Ticknor, a very large man past middle age who had settled in the bush country near Nelson. He was a skilled naturalist and hunter – and somewhat eccentric. He captured two young elk, which he raised and broke to harness. Then Tom, arrayed in skin garments topped with a wolfhide hat, the tail hanging down his back, drove his unique team around the countryside. For variety – or perhaps in a fit of sociability – he met one of the first trains on the newly-completed line to Morden, 12.5 km (8 miles) south of Nelson. Here he entertained astonished passengers with a wild dance accompanied by blood-curdling war whoops.

Another notable district resident, though for a different reason, was H.J. Borthwick. He was one of the earliest missionaries to serve an area which included not only Nelson but also twenty-nine other congregations. He covered his huge territory of 8,000 square km (3,000 square miles) driving a buckboard drawn by his old horse, Tom. This rugged pair travelled thousands of miles, endured summer storms and winter blizzards, taking shelter at night on the lee side of a straw-stack if no settler's home was near. Then a brick church was built in Nelsonville in 1881, with others soon following. The churches lessened hardships of the early missionaries such as Borthwick, although they still regularly visited their scattered parishioners.

Sadly for Nelson, the optimism shown by the erection of churches and other buildings proved unfounded. In 1883 the CPR's Pembina Branch line was built and missed Nelson by 12.5 km (8 miles). The town was doomed since a new community, Morden; appeared on the railway line. By 1885, Nelson was literally disappearing down the road as building after building was hauled south to the new town.

J.H. Fraser moved his mill there while the Nelson Mills went to Mountain City. Maple Leaf school and two of the churches were relocated in Morden, the third was sold to the Mennonites who tore it down and reused the material. They also bought the town hall for the same purpose. Completion of the railway brought them another bonus – without traffic, Billy Brown's hated Halfway House and its evil liquor passed into folklore.

Nelson followed. Today a cairn is all that remains of a once bustling and optimistic prairie community.

NORQUAY AND LITTLETON

MANY TOWN SITES HAD THEIR BEGINNINGS on a water source in order to facilitate milling operations. Norquay and Littleton were no exception, both having their genesis on the Cypress River during the 1880s.

Norquay was named after Sir John Norquay, then premier of Manitoba. In 1880, Dr. J.P. Pennefather purchased a section of land from the Hudson's Bay Company for five dollars an acre. It was located four miles north of Swan Lake and, since this area had already been surveyed for a rail line, settlers felt safe in assuming it would come their way. This being the mood of the day, the town began with the building of a store and post office by W.H. Pentland and Charles Holland, named, appropriately, Holland and Pentland.

Dr. Pennefather, in his book, *Thirteen Years on the Prairie*, published in 1892, noted that the store was an excellent one: "A good deal of their business is carried on in trade or farm produce which is generally shipped into Winnipeg for sale. Luxuries as well as necessities of all kinds are to be had."

A.K. Berry in his book, *Reflections 1881-1937*, also mentions the store saying it, "…kept very few things for women or children because eight or nine out of every ten settlers was a bachelor." Fat pork in brine, called 'mess pork' was a popular seller and was available by the barrel. Hardware was not stocked, though, which seems an odd omission for a town under construction.

A stopping house built in 1881 by Edwin Sparling for a Cockney named Prior was named Norquay Hotel and was considered to be a "very fair establishment."

Mr. Sparling also built the stone press mill. When the machinery for its construction arrived in Emerson, it required the efforts of every available ox team in the settlement to haul it to the site on the north bank of the Cypress River. The grist mill soon became busy with farmers coming long distances to have their wheat ground for flour and oats and barley for feed.

Along with the grist mill, a saw mill was soon in production and, Dr. Pennefather wrote: "…the difficulties of procuring provisions and lumber ceased before we were eighteen months in this country." Things were looking up.

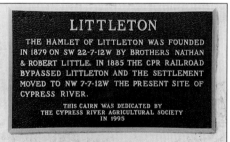

LITTLETON

THE HAMLET OF LITTLETON WAS FOUNDED IN 1879 ON SW 22-7-12W BY BROTHERS NATHAN & ROBERT LITTLE. IN 1885 THE CPR RAILROAD BYPASSED LITTLETON AND THE SETTLEMENT MOVED TO NW 7-7-12W THE PRESENT SITE OF CYPRESS RIVER.

THIS CAIRN WAS DEDICATED BY THE CYPRESS RIVER AGRICULTURAL SOCIETY IN 1995

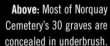

Above: Most of Norquay Cemetery's 30 graves are concealed in underbrush.

Right: A settler's pride and joy – a handsome team of horses.

A.K Berry, a butcher by trade, took logs to the sawmill to have them made into lumber for the construction of his home a few miles from the village. An entrepreneur at heart, he could see the possibilities of a future in the meat trade so he built a combined shop and slaughter-house in Norquay. In September of 1881, when Berry killed his first beef, he was swamped with customers who hadn't had a taste of fresh meat for six months.

Business continued brisk and he also went about the countryside plying his trade. He charged two dollars for slaughtering and dressing an animal, or the hide, in lieu of cash. He often opted for taking the hide as payment in that cash-scarce economy.

For some, cash was scarcer than for others and, according to Mr. Berry, one settler tried a unique method to avoid payment of his debts. This man had run up a bill of fifteen dollars at the butcher shop, but agreed to supply Berry with a heifer to satisfy the debt. When Berry asked the man to bring the animal to him, however, he was adamant in his refusal and quoted scripture to support his case. "The cattle on the hill are the Lord's," he maintained.

Not to be put off by the man's "spell of religious mania," Berry took matters into his own hands and secured the heifer for himself. Then he made out a statement and mailed it to the farmer. A reply came a few days later: "One heifer, stolen from Christ the Son of God. May God have mercy on your soul." Berry stood firm and that issue was eventually resolved, but the 'Christian' settler was undeterred by his failure to outwit the butcher. He gave the ploy another try at one of the grocery stores. "The Lord will pay for my goods," he promised, but the owner saw no reason to count on that possibility and the man was encouraged to move to another town.

The School District of Norquay was formed in 1883. And, according to Dr. Pennefather, there were other 'useful' additions to the community. One of these was a tailor from England by the name of Mr. Newbury Sr. Another was a Dr. Baldwin who arrived in 1883 to homestead.

A.K. Berry's description of the doctor, however, gives the impression that his expertise was less than useful. When Dr. Baldwin was called to assist in the birth of

Berry's daughter, "(he) was not in a fit state to attend anyone and fell in a drunken stupor across the foot of the bed." Luckily, Mrs. Pennycook, a Scottish neighbour with nurse's training, was on hand to take over.

Perhaps a lack of tailoring business inspired Mr. Newbury's son to look to other means of support, for he started a tinsmith shop. By 1881, Wm. Brown was operating a wagon and blacksmith business and the community felt reasonably independent.

Presbyterians and Methodists held services in homes on alternate Sundays and the nearest Roman Catholic priest resided about fifteen miles away in the village of St. Leon. But, according to Dr. Pennefather, Episcopalian (Anglican) clergy never came near the settlement. Members of that denomination, somewhat aggrieved by the slight, sought to correct it by building a rectory. About 1884, their mission completed, the first clergyman, Rev. William Barbour, took up residence. His tenure was short-lived, though, when it became clear that sufficient funds to pay his salary were unavailable. Failure to take this ongoing cost into account was a curious oversight, considering the eagerness with which the settlement's Anglicans yearned for their own church.

Although the Lorne Agricultural Society was organized in Norquay, the village survived just long enough to host one fair. A delegation from the Lorne Municipality was sent to confer with incorporate railways in Winnipeg to see on what terms any of them might consider building a line through Norquay. The municipality was to provide a bonus of $65,000. There were no takers, however, and the village, like so many others, lost hope.

Businesses and residents moved out. Holland and Pentland relocated their store to Holland and Mr. Berry did likewise with his butcher shop. The Anglican rectory was moved to Somerset, used until 1955 and later demolished. When the mill was dismantled, nothing was left of the dream that was Norquay.

The casual explorer might be forgiven for missing them completely, but landmarks for the second location of the Norquay School and Cemetery can still be found. The latter, located one half mile from the original town site, contains only four accessible graves. The balance – some thirty in number – are concealed in underbrush, and markers have disintegrated with the passage of years.

LITTLETON'S history began in 1879, following Norquay's demise, and was named for brothers, Nathaniel and Robert Little. Littleton also overlooked the Cypress River. By 1881 mail service had been established and a school, named Selton opened. This was the first school built in the Cypress River area. Although not a lot is known about this settlement, the Holland History (1967) mentions two churches – Methodist and Presbyterian – a hotel, general store, saw mill, shingle mill, blacksmith and livery stable. A doctor and carpenter were in residence as well.

While it seemed that enough settlers and businesses were in place to ensure an ongoing and prosperous community, the railroad, as usual, spelled its doom. A delegation met with representatives from the Manitoba South Western Colonization Railway hoping to acquire service to their town. Their hopes were dashed, however, when the rail line took a more southerly route. When the town of Cypress River, which had been surveyed in 1896, began to grow, Littleton's fate was sealed and most of it relocated there.

WHILE IT SEEMED THAT ENOUGH SETTLERS AND BUSINESSES WERE IN PLACE TO ENSURE AN ONGOING AND PROSPEROUS COMMUNITY, THE RAILROAD, AS USUAL, SPELLED ITS DOOM.

Below: Homesteaders trekking westward.

ODANAH

Right: A rubble-filled basement in Odanah.

ODANAH, FROM THE CREE WORD "OTANOW," has been variously translated as a "meeting place," a "resting place" and a "gathering place." Whatever the origin, it was the name given to a Cree winter encampment nestled between the Little Saskatchewan (now Minnedosa) River and the foothills of the Riding Mountains.

The area was still part of the North-West Territories when a surge of settlement in 1879 necessitated building a Land Titles Office at the site of the Cree encampment. Then a post office was established, streets laid out and the village of Odanah born. Soon business enterprises included two general stores, a hardware store, sawmill and even a photography studio.

Meanwhile, a rival settlement about 2 km (1 mile) to the east was established where a trail crossed the river. First called Tanner's Crossing, it soon became known as Minnedosa. During 1882-83 the area boomed, with lots between the two settlements eagerly bought by speculators. But those who had wagered that Odanah would win the townsite rivalry suffered a defeat in 1883. Minnedosa was incorporated into a town and its

boundaries included Odanah. Then the Manitoba and North Western Railway located its station at Minnedosa and there was no doubt which townsite would survive. By 1885, Odanah's businesses had all moved to Minnedosa. Only the name remains – and that because it was given to the surrounding municipality.

Although no one remembers Odanah Village, the site is not entirely obliterated. Amid the Manitoba maples, elm, chokecherry, cranberry and hawthorn bushes the remains of a basement or two hide beneath a wild tangle of undergrowth. In addition, a commemorative plaque notes: "1878 ODANAH 1886: This plaque erected in 1967 on the site of the Carlton Trail, through Odanah Village and the Pass."

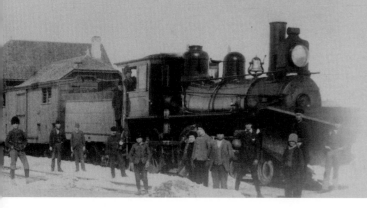

OLD DAUPHIN
AND GARTMORE

WITH THE BIRTH OF THE TOWN OF DAUPHIN IN 1896 the lives of two nearby villages ended and with them the spirited rivalry that had enlivened their existence from the beginning. Old Dauphin, just north of the present town, and Gartmore, some 5 km (3 miles) to the southwest, competed for everything from customers for their tea, tin, and tobacco emporiums to overnight guests at leading hotels. In Dauphin the Dauphin House modestly noted that it was "conveniently located to all the principal business places in town," while the International in Gartmore assured its guests "moderate rates" and "good stable in connection." But, most of all, the towns competed for the terminus of the railway. Ironically, the railway was ultimately to kill them both.

Old Dauphin and Gartmore were born in 1886 and 1889 to serve the needs of early settlers in the Dauphin Valley. Until 1883 this remote area between the Duck and Riding Mountains was familiar only to wandering Aboriginal bands and a few Métis families who lived on the shores of Lake Dauphin. In June of that year, however, Thomas Whitmore of Gladstone organized a party of men to search for a beautiful valley that had been described to him by one of the Metis from the lake.

With teams of horses and oxen the explorers skirted Riding Mountain, crossed the Ochre River and pushed farther west. One of the men, John Edwards, stopped at the banks of a creek later named for him to plant a crop of potatoes. He then went back to Gladstone for his family and returned in the fall to become the first white settler in the area. Other members of the party continued on to the Vermillion River where they marked land claims by blazing trees before returning to Gladstone.

Later that summer, Neil McDonald of Woodside and his sons followed the trail of the Whitmore party and claimed land nearby. The following spring, however, when they tried to return to the Dauphin Valley by the same route, they found it had been made impassable by heavy rains. Instead, they hacked their way along an old Aboriginal trail over the mountain and so opened another route for settlers.

By 1886 well over a dozen families lived in the district. Among them was David McIntosh who opened a store on his homestead, which became the nucleus of the village of Old Dauphin, also known as Dog Town, but just why is a mystery. A magistrate, constable and

**BY 1886 WELL
OVER A DOZEN
FAMILIES LIVED
IN THE DISTRICT.**

HER MAJESTY'S
MAIL – AND
POSTMASTER
MCINTOSH –
WERE THREATENED
BY FLOOD RIVERS,
WASHED-OUT
BRIDGES, MUSKEG
AND GUMBO MUD.

Below: Clearing the land.

bailiff were appointed and the village soon had two blacksmith shops and a variety of other business places, including a hotel, several general stores and a doctor's office and pharmacy. Two churches were built and a newspaper, The Dauphin Pioneer-Press, began publishing in April 1896.

Gartmore developed in similar fashion, getting its start when the Hudson's Bay Company moved its store close to one already built on Tom Whitmore's land. Although both villages eventually acquired post offices, until 1890 settlers had to depend upon infrequent visitors to carry in letters and newspapers.

There was an improvement in mail delivery after 1890 when the Dominion government built what was called a road, although one resident, David McIntosh, on many occasions had other names for it. He was Old Dauphin's first postmaster; his duties included driving a four-horse stagecoach over the hazardous route. Each spring, Her Majesty's mail – and postmaster McIntosh – were threatened by flooding rivers, washed-out bridges, muskeg and gumbo mud. One of McIntosh's successors, mail driver Samuel Chatwin, encountered another hazard. One year he spent more than his total salary to rent extra horses and hire men who would

help repair bridges and make floats so that he could cross the swollen rivers to more or less maintain the mail schedule.

Lack of good roads and a railway during the first decade of settlement kept the area in isolation and forced farmers to grow only enough produce for their own needs. There was no doubt, however, that the fertile Dauphin Valley could produce much more. J.B. Tyrell, sent by the Dominion government in 1887 to examine the potential of the area, called it one of the best and surest mixed farming districts in western Canada. Part of his report is in the book, *Dauphin Valley Spans The Years,* published by the Dauphin Historical Society. "The rich grasses and the pure water make it the natural home for stock," he noted, "and the deep rich soil yields the very heaviest crops of cereals, roots and vegetables."

Small fruits also thrived, dairying was profitable, and a successful bee-keeping industry started in 1884 when Alfred Maynard brought a hive with him from Ontario. A flour mill established in 1890 enabled settlers to grind their own wheat and a saw mill in connection led to the development of a sizeable lumbering business. All that was needed to ensure further growth, everyone agreed, was rail access to the outside markets.

Six more years of isolation passed before the railway become a reality – with disastrous consequences to the pioneer communities. In April 1896 William MacKenzie and Donald Mann acquired the charter of the Lake Manitoba Railway and Canal Company and began construction of the long-awaited railway to Dauphin. As the first rails were laid at Gladstone towards the settlement in the Dauphin Valley the guessing games began – which village would get the station? Various newspapers of the day predicted that neither village would get it and, furthermore, that they had only themselves to blame. "Between the villages of Dauphin and Gartmore there exists a spirit of rivalry and jealousy that has proven fatal to many Manitoba towns," ran a squib that appeared in several publications during the summer of 1896. "They are squabbling for the terminus of the railway and the difficulty is likely to be settled by placing the station midway between the two."

This prediction proved true. The railway decided to locate between the two villages, dooming both fledgling towns. *The Dauphin Pioneer-Press*, however, noted that the decision was not the result of a squabble but was simply an attempt by railway officials to "strike a location suitable to most people while not overlooking the needs of the road, and at the same time not to create any ill-feeling.

"There is small choice between the various sites on the east side of the Vermillion, all being very good," the paper commented in its September 9, 1896, edition. "The final settlement of the vexed question will be hailed with delight."

Indeed, the establishment of the new town of Dauphin and the subsequent migration from the old villages was accomplished with minimum delay and apparent good humour. Buildings were moved sometimes with amusing results. On November 4, 1896, the *Pioneer-Press* reported: "Clark's Hotel began to move on Friday morning before the hour at which one of the star board-

ers usually rises. When he awoke the unwonted motion made him so sea-sick that he kept to his bed all day."

A further item reveals that the hotel didn't reach the new town until Monday, its progress having been impeded by soft snow. On the other hand the paper later noted that the snow facilitated the removal of a building from Gartmore: "On Friday…the old-time 'Department of Education' was moved to the new town, being placed on Main St. nearly opposite Mr. McLean's hotel. The trip was made in about an hour and a half, four teams drawing it on skids, the light snow being just the thing for that." The report goes on to add: "Mr. Farrer is having it snugly fitted up and will continue the stationery and fancy goods business in it."

By December 9 the newspaper was able to relate that changes wrought in the Dauphin townsite "down all previous records in the line of town building in this country. The plain unvarnished tale of progress made in converting a level stubble field into a town with several blocks of buildings closely built would rival the Arabian Nights."

Above: A lonely vigil.

By this time the first telegraphic dispatch had been sent to cities all over the world announcing that the space between Dauphin and the outside world had been "annihilated," that Dauphin now had both railway and telegraphic communication with the "outside" world. In fact the first load of wheat had already been marketed and shipped by rail from Dauphin. Finally, on December 15, 1896, the first passenger train steamed into town and the transformation was complete. The years of isolation were over, rivalry was put aside, and the frontier villages of Gartmore and Old Dauphin passed into memory.

OLD DELORAINE

BECAUSE A CLEARER, MORE PERMANENT MARKING of the boundary between Canada and the United States was needed, the Boundary Commission began work to establish a recognizable border. They used an old Aboriginal trail stretching from Emerson west to the Rocky Mountains, and completed the project in 1874. This important new road was used by the Northwest Mounted Police in their quest to bring law and order to the new nation. It also provided a supply route over which new settlers travelled to the Turtle Mountain area in search of available good, cheap land.

Many of the settlers had come north through the United States to Emerson and then made the difficult trip west in covered wagons. Others, however, chose a different route, using stern wheeler flat-bottomed boats on the Assiniboine River to the junction of the Souris and Assiniboine. From there, they were obliged to transport themselves and their effects to the Deloraine settlement via the Brandon or Heaslip Trail. That route was also used for freighting and to carry mail by stage coach from Brandon to Deloraine.

In 1880, in order to serve the influx of settlers, a Land Titles Office was built at the junctions of Turtle Head Creek and the Boundary Commission and Mandan trails. Today, a replica of the office stands at that location and nearby, faint remnants of the old Boundary Commission Trail can still be detected.

A settlement began a short distance away, which according to the *Geographical Place Names of Manitoba* was originally called Zulu. This may have been a joke perpetrated by the *Brandon Mail's* editor. In any case the name, Deloraine, was ultimately chosen by James Cavers after his home town in Scotland. He also ran the general store which was built in 1883 and housed the post office. Building proceeded apace and, besides dwellings, the town soon had a gristmill, two blacksmiths, a machinery business, a physician, law office and a bank. The bank vault, made of fieldstone and restored in the 1970s, still stands proud, secure and very lonely in a farmer's field.

Opposite: Bank vault still standing in a farmer's field near Deloraine.

Above: Faint remnants still exist of the Boundary Commission Trail.

Right: Replica of the Land Titles office at the junction of Turtle Head Creek and the Mandan and Boundary Commission Trails.

As was the custom of the times, the first church services were conducted in various homes and later, in the school. When a building was erected, the parsonage was on the ground floor with the sanctuary upstairs.

The town hall was rented for fifty dollars per year for use as a school and classes began there May first in 1884. School was in session only during the more temperate months, suspended during the harsh Prairie winters, and reopened in the spring.

As happened so often in the early days of settlement, the expected railway missed the little town site. It went, instead, four and a half miles to the northwest. So Old Deloraine citizens simply waited until there was snow on the ground and, in 1886, skidded the entire town to 'new' Deloraine.

Even before settlement began in the area, coal had been discovered in the Turtle Mountains near the Boundary Commission Trail. According to A.D. Doerkson's writings in *The Saga Of Turtle Mountain Coal*,

it was in 1879 that the 'black diamonds' were first turned up by an early settler during the digging of a water well. At a depth of thirty feet, he uncovered a three foot seam and, when tried as a fuel, it proved to be very satisfactory. Other finds followed and, by 1883, coal was being mined commercially with some of the settlers finding employment in the business. In spite of high hopes, however, the coal boom never happened, although a number of mines were in operation and supplied settlers with cheap fuel for a time. Hopes were revived during the Great Depression of the 1930s when crop failures plagued the prairies. Several mines offered coal at $2.25 a ton 'cash and carry,' a blessing to cash strapped families. In spite of large deposits known to be in the area, coal mining in south western Manitoba was pretty much limited to local consumption and never exploited to the degree it might have been.

Many of the pioneers who lived through the colourful early years of settlement in this beautiful part of Manitoba were laid to rest in the Old Deloraine Cemetery. It is a lovingly tended, peaceful spot located about a half-mile south of the old Boundary Commission Trail.

OLD STOCKTON, STOCKTON AND HILTON

RESIDENTS OF MANY PIONEER MANITOBA COMMUNITIES needed a character trait additional to their ability to adapt to loneliness, isolation and adversity. This trait was flexibility since changing circumstances frequently forced them to move not only themselves but their settlements as well – usually to the nearest railway. Old Stockton, however, added a variation. It was not only moved, but went in two different directions.

Its problem occurred in 1890 when the Northern Pacific Railway completed a line to Brandon and began a daily service to Belmont and Baldur. Trains carried mixed freight south and returned at night with grain, milk, cattle and other agricultural products. This system took care of most of the settlers' needs and the services available in Old Stockton were no longer required.

Its post office, known as Thorsby, was moved north to the Manitoba South Western Colonization Railway's northern line and the name changed to Stockton. Other buildings soon followed. The April 18, 1891, issue of the *Brandon Sun* reported: "The old town of Stockton…is being moved…eight miles west of Glenboro. The town is situated within a mile of the Assiniboine and the stream at this point has considerable fall; the banks are also favourable for building a water power plant. It is one of the best locations for a grist mill in Manitoba and there is still no mill nearer than 22 miles. The soil is very early here and No. 1 wheat can be grown nine times out

of ten. Good water is obtained at 25 feet and wood is abundant and convenient."

Only ten days later the same paper optimistically reviewed the results of the move: "Stockton of three months is booming still. Mr. Abbot is erecting a handsome dwelling and in connection a commodious office for general insurance and real estate, etc."

The boom continued until the town had almost two dozen businesses offering goods and services. There was also a physician and a jeweller who extracted teeth as a sideline. As was the case in all pioneer communities, townspeople organized various Lodges and Societies and in 1896 constructed an outdoor rink for curling and skating. The *Glenboro Gazette* reported: "January 2nd turned out to be one of the coldest days of the year with a blizzard raging out of the north. Every able bodied man turned out to flood the rink."

The same enterprising spirit was evident nearly half a century later when another rink was needed. On December 8, 1938, the *Glenboro Gazette* noted:

THE BOOM CONTINUED UNTIL THE TOWN HAD ALMOST TWO DOZEN BUSINESSES OFFERING GOODS AND SERVICES.

"Curling history was made at Stockton last Thursday when the official opening of the new rink took place. The rink itself is probably the only one of its kind in Manitoba, for when those interested in the sport found it impossible to build a proper rink they borrowed a hay baler and baled straw and constructed walls of the material. The roof is of heavy poles, covered with long marsh hay, while the windows are covered with flour sacks. A well was dug inside the rink, which houses one good sheet of ice. It was in this building, which cost nothing but labour, the official opening took place, between World Champion Ab Gowanlock and a Stockton rink under Dolph Sampson."

But by now the frontier era was well past and the process of church and school consolidation, along with better roads and transportation, took people to larger centres such as Glenboro, Wawanesa and Brandon. Without this trade the business community of Stockton died. Some residents remained, however, and new ones arrived, although not the traditional young people looking for a new frontier. They were elderly citizens who chose to spend their retirement years in this pleasant small community.

Stockton's sister village of Hilton was also born in 1890 when the building of a line south of Brandon by the Northern Pacific Railway killed Old Stockton. The por-

Below: Scottish crofters settled the area two years before the village of Hilton appeared.

WE'RE SAILING WEST, WE'RE SAILING WEST, TO PRAIRIE LANDS SUNKISSED AND BLEST- THE CROFTER'S TRAIL TO HAPPINESS.

tion of Old Stockton not absorbed by Stockton was moved south and became part of the village of Hilton. "The railway giveth and the railway taketh away," was the way many residents resignedly summarized the situation.

As soon as the railway completed its line to Hilton, the Manitoba Elevator Company built an elevator. It was followed by other business enterprises, including two more elevators. By the mid 1890s the community had a population of approximately 200. Two years before the village was established, the area was settled by Scottish crofters and one of the terms of settlement was that they be provided with church services in Gaelic. So for the first few years ministers had to be able to speak both English and Gaelic. Services were held in homes and halls, since no church was erected until the turn of the century.

Hilton's importance as a trading centre lasted less than ten years. In 1898 the Northern Pacific and Manitoba Railway Company completed a branch line between Hartney and Ninette, cutting off trade from the south. The railway had again "taken away." The leave-taking began once more, buildings being moved to begin life anew on nearby farms. Eventually, the one elevator to escape destruction found a new home in Ninette.

But the spirit of a community dies hard, especially Hilton's. A few people stayed and a store and post office remained in operation. In 1961, a new village hall, built by energetic volunteers, provided a community centre

for dances and bingo, with the revenue used to pay off the mortgage. In 1970, there was still enough enthusiasm in the surrounding community to celebrate Manitoba's Centennial with a homecoming dinner and a tree planting ceremony. But Hilton nevertheless withered like Old Stockton and Stockton.

The store and post office closed and by 1980 only a few people remained. One was Mr. Notman who remembered the community when it was alive with people and sports such as curling, tennis, football and skating were popular. But the biggest source of pride was the local racetrack. "It was just south of the village," he recalled, "and it was a good half-mile track. Hilton was a busy place then with horses coming from all over – some from the States, too.

"But now," he said sadly, "now it's just part of a farm; just another field."

Left: Early grain elevators.

Above: Once Hilton was alive with people but today is virtually deserted.

OLHA, SEECH AND HOROD

UKRAINIAN MIGRATION TO WESTERN CANADA, which began in the late 1890s, was instigated by Dr. Oleskiw who was a Professor of Agriculture in Lemburg, Austria. Concerned by the fact that the peasants in Ukraine (then under Austrian rule) were kept from owning land, and their children deprived of an education, he contacted the Department of the Interior in Ottawa regarding opportunities in Canada. In 1895, he came to Manitoba to study its potential for immigration. Upon his return home, Dr. Oleskiw published a book and pamphlets, which spurred interest among people from Galicia and Bukovina. In correspondence with Sir Clifford Sifton, he stated that at least two hundred families would come to Canada.

HERE THE SETTLERS WERE OBLIGED TO LIVE IN TENTS UNDER QUARANTINE WHILE THEIR POTENTIAL HOME-STEADS WERE BEING SURVEYED.

The first large contingent arrived in Strathclair, Manitoba in May 1899 under harrowing circumstances. After sailing from Hamburg to Halifax in the hold of the ship under poor conditions, they arrived in Winnipeg by train. There they stopped long enough to acquire seed potatoes and a few other necessities before proceeding west and north. Only a few miles out of Portage la Prairie, however, three children died from a virulent strain of scarlet fever and were buried by the train tracks at Strathclair. More and more people sickened – mainly children. An epidemic was in progress.

According to the Oakburn Centennial history book, *Echoes*, the shelter at Strathclair (such as it was)

HOROD
1899 — 1999

IN 1899, 214 PEOPLE FROM THE WESTERN
UKRAINE SETTLED IN AN AREA SOUTH OF
THE RIDING MOUNTAINS, A REGION CHOSEN
FOR ITS ABUNDANCE OF WATER, WOOD
AND HAY. TOILING ON THEIR 160-ACRE
HOMESTEADS, THEY CREATED A
COMMUNITY CALLED HOROD, NAMED AFTER
A VILLAGE IN THEIR NATIVE LAND.
AT ITS PEAK, HOROD CONSISTED OF A
SCHOOL, CREATED IN 1906, A CHURCH
BUILT IN 1923, A STORE AND POST-
OFFICE OPENED IN 1925, AND A HALL
IN 1936.
ERECTED IN 1999 IN TRIBUTE TO THE
PIONEERS WHOSE SUCCESS IN CREATING
A COMMUNITY IS STILL EVIDENT IN
THE PRESENCE OF THE SCHOOL, CHURCH
AND HALL.

consisted of two unheated buildings with a scattering of hay on the floor. Cooking was done outdoors over an open fire. During the stay there, several more children died, but one mother, Mrs. Swystun, who wanted her baby buried near where the family would be home-steading, kept its death secret and cradled the child in her arms during the wagon trip to Patterson Lake in the Olha District.

Here the settlers were obliged to live in tents under quarantine while their potential homesteads were being surveyed. Conditions were abysmal. Everyone was drenched with a cold rain before the tents were erected and, although stoves had been set up inside, dry kindling was difficult to find. There was little food and the fami-

lies had to sleep on the frozen ground covered only with a thin layer of hay.

During that first night, a late snowstorm covered the area, most of the rest of the children sickened and many began to die. The chain of death continued for two weeks during which forty-two children and three adults succumbed. Adults were better able to fend off the disease, but only four children survived the ordeal and all of the families suffered losses. A more tragic beginning to life in Canada can hardly be imagined.

A monument to honour the deceased now stands near the large mound that contains the forty-five bodies from that terrible time.

Each adult male settler was granted 160 acres of land (a quarter section) and was required to work it for three years before he could acquire title. Having a son at least sixteen years of age provided settlers with the option of obtaining an additional 160 acres. Also, settlers were allowed to purchase a quarter section 'pre-exemption grant' at a cost of one dollar per acre, which could be paid in installments if necessary. It, too, had to be paid in the three-year time period in order to obtain title. At the end of this time, most of the settlers had paid their ten dollars per grant and become British Subjects.

After homesteads were allotted, the next step was to erect a temporary shelter. A shallow depression approximately four feet deep was dug into the ground and the structure of poles built over it was then thatched. According to a history of Ukrainian settlement, *From The Past To The Present 1898-1987*, these crude huts were called 'buddas' and served until more substantial homes could be built. Because the area was heavily wooded, the next dwelling was often made of logs plastered with a mud and straw mix and roofed with straw thatch. When saw mills became operational nearby, frame houses were the choice of construction.

At the outset, furniture as well as dwellings, had to be built using wooden pegs since nails were not available. Mattresses were made of canvas and filled with straw. Early settlers seldom had cooking stoves, so an outdoor oven (pietz) was constructed with willows bent into a horseshoe shape and placed over a base made of a clay and straw mix. Then the walls were plastered inside and out with about six inches of the same clay mixture.

Left: Ukrainian Greek Orthodox Church at Seech.

Above: Replica of a *budda*, an early Ukrainian shelter that served until more substantial homes could be built.

In spite of early difficulties and hardships, the industrious Ukrainians managed to forge out successful lives on the forested slopes of the Riding Mountains. Backbreaking toil was the order of the day when clearing land for crops and, to their disappointment, seed wheat brought from the Ukraine wasn't sufficiently hardy for use in Manitoba and the first crops froze. Later, in the Seech district, Peter Peech and several others grew Red Fyfe wheat, which proved to be satisfactory and it was distributed for seed. Even so, the business of sowing grain by hand and harvesting with sickle and flail was no easy task. Many of the farmers and older boys had to

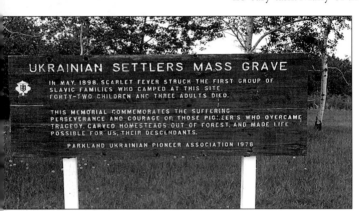

find outside employment in order to make money – some worked for more established farmers while others got jobs on the railroad. Wives and children were left to manage the homesteads – sometimes for months at a stretch – and they had the responsibility of breaking land for gardens and tending whatever fowl or animals they possessed. Meat, usually wild game, had to be smoke or brine cured, mushrooms picked and dried, fruit gathered and soap made. The harder labour was left until the men returned in the fall and, in addition to clearing more land, they cut and hauled wood for fuel. Extra cordwood was taken to Shoal Lake and sold for cash needed to purchase household supplies.

The hamlet of Olha was named for a Russian princess and saint who reigned from 945 to 964 A.D., one of the first of her dynasty to become Christian. The first post office opened there in 1908 in the farm home of a Dmytro Luhowy. In 1910, Hnat Budiwski took it over, but since he had to seek work elsewhere, his wife assumed the duties of mail delivery. No easy task, for she had to walk twice a week to Oakburn for the mail and

then deliver it – a distance of about 16 km (10 miles) one way.

Because educating the children was an important aspiration, the establishment of schools was a priority and one was built at Olha in 1907. Seech, which translates as 'battle' in the Ukrainian/English dictionary, and was named to honour Zaporozian Seech in Greater Ukraine, began settlement in 1900. The school, opened there in 1910, was not large enough to accommodate the eighty children who enrolled and the younger pupils had to make do with benches since there weren't enough desks to go around.

Horod, north of Elphinstone, was named for a village in Ukraine, and the Ukrainian/English dictionary translates the word as 'garden'. The book, *Readings In Ukrainian Authors* edited by C.H. Andrusyshen, however, states that Horod was the name given to embattlements built by Cossacks as protection against the Tartars. In any event, the first school, was ready for classes in 1909, but in 1930 it was moved two and one half miles north east of its original site. Since carefully restored, the school as well as the teacherage is open to the public.

Adversity and hard work were no strangers to these first immigrants whose faith gave them hope for a better future. The many churches built in the ensuing years are a testament to their tenacity. Places of worship were also a cultural connection to their homeland and an important centre for social activities, particularly during religious holidays. The legacy left behind can be seen, not only in the large numbers of churches erected, but also in the variety of architecture and ornamentation.

In the beginning, Seech area residents congregated outdoors where a bell, brought from the Ukraine was hung between two spruce trees. When St. Michael's Church was built at Olha in 1904, it also served the Seech congregation until they built St. Mary's Church in 1912. Others in the Seech district – people of the Ukrainian Greek Orthodox faith – began meeting in homes in 1936 and by 1942 had erected their own building. Horod's Holy Eucharist Ukrainian Catholic Church was built in 1922.

Although Horod, Seech and Olha were really just hamlets, each having little more than a church, store, post office and community hall, they and other villages like them were an important part of early settlement. They were the places where people could meet, worship, purchase necessities and hold meetings, dances or entertainments such as dramatic presentations. As with other pioneers, many of the earliest parties were held in homes with local musicians supplying the music.

At some of these gatherings, Mike Swystun (sometimes spelled Swistun) a local character from Olha, who was a son of the first immigrants, performed sleight of hand magic as well as hypnosis. Mike, whose feats of strength were legendary, worked for Barnum and Bailey for some time where he was billed as the World's Strongest Man. He had trained himself by lifting bags of grain with his teeth, then progressing to heavier and heavier weights until he could bend steel bars with his teeth. The strong man's international reputation, however, wasn't always appreciated on his own turf. Neighbours regarded his tricks and ability to induce hypnotic spells as a kind of sorcery and some called him a devil. They didn't, for example, enjoy the sight of him pounding a nail through the back of his head and bringing it out through his nose, and there were those who mistook the illusion for reality.

It was Swystun's ability to hypnotize, though, that is best remembered by many people in the area. At a social event, Swystun put several ladies in a trance. When he persuaded them that they were wading through deep water, they lifted their skirts – scandalous behaviour in that decorous age! The incident is still recalled with some amusement by the locals.

One of the school teachers at Olha was the multi-talented Jacob Maydanyk. In the early 1920s under his direction, a hundred dollars worth of second hand books were acquired and a reading association and lending library established. The books were first stored at the school where people met in the evenings for readings or to borrow books, but in 1936 when the Olha hall was built, the association moved there. Maydanyk was also an artist and painted the interior of St. Michael's Church and was probably the artist responsible for painting the backdrops in the Olha hall, which was used for the many dramatic productions. His life and times were documented by the National Film Board in a production called Laughter In My Soul. Although no one was sure of his religion or politics, Maydanyk chronicled the lives of early Ukrainian pioneers in books. Many of his readers could also relate to, and delight in, the antics of his wonderful cartoon character, Shteef Tabachiuk, featured in Ukrainian periodicals.

These early settlements, small as they were, followed the pattern of others when larger farms, smaller populations and school consolidations took people to larger centres to do their business. The Olha General Store, however, remains in business to provide a few groceries, confectionery and a large fund of information. Mrs. Marion Koltusky, the genial proprietor, is able and very willing to accommodate visitors eager to learn something of the history of the area. She is proud to escort them on a tour of the beautiful St. Michael's Church and lovingly tended graveyard where the earliest of the Ukrainian pioneers now rest.

Above: A 'pietz' – Ukrainian outdoor oven.

Below: Starting a new life in Canada.

POLONIA

POLONIA OR HUN'S VALLEY, AS IT ONCE WAS KNOWN, came to life as the result of a colonization project initiated by Hungarian aristocrat Paul Oscar Esterhazy. His assistant and countryman, agriculturist Geza Stephen de Dory led the first seventeen families to this beautiful valley in 1885.

Even today, a visit to this almost hidden area 26 km (16 miles) northwest of Neepawa offers a feast for the eyes as well as a glimpse into the lives of those early settlers. A country road leads west from Highway 5, past rolling farmland and deep into a valley, patch-worked in fertile shades of green and gold. The spire of a blue-roofed church and a cluster of white build-ings, toy-like when viewed from above, indicate what remains of the village.

Here stands a century old church named for St. Elizabeth of Hungary. Beside it is the community hall, built in 1940 as a parish hall and renovated several times since. Among the flowers and well-kept lawns of the churchyard are Stations of the Cross and beyond them, a stone grotto built by parishioners in 1959 under the direction of their parish priest, Reverend W. Plucinski, to honour the one hundredth anniversary of the visions at Lourdes.

Although the church is no longer in regular Sunday use, it continues as a centre of Marian devotion. A repli-ca of a painting of Our Lady of Czestochowa, also called the Black Madonna, hangs over the altar. Tradition says the original was painted on a cypress table top by Saint Luke the Evangelist during the lifetime of Mary, moth-er of Jesus. Its brown tints have deepened with time, hence the term Black Madonna. The painting was brought to Constantinople from the Holy Land by Saint Helen, mother of Constantine the Great and eventually taken to a monastery on Jasna Gora (Bright Hill) at Czcestochowa in Poland. It has undergone three restora-tions, the last by Professor John Rutkowski who also painted the picture that hangs in St. Elizabeth's Church.

Each year on the third Sunday of July, descendents of the Polish settlers and others from around the province gather at Polonia for the annual pilgrimage. The church is also open for special services at Christmas.

Cindy (Kolesar) Williams recalls taking part in the pilgrimages each year when she was growing up on the family farm three miles south of the village. "I don't remember that it ever rained on the day of the pilgrimage," she remarks. "Not once in all those years."

Some of the children wore Polish costumes for the event. "Father Plucinscki brought them back with him from Poland," says Williams. "The skirts were made of wool and they were hot and uncomfortable!" But that

Opposite: Joe Terlecki's store, opened in 1927, became a popular gathering place.

Above: G.S. de Dory's log home at Hun's Valley.

Right: A country road leads deep into the valley at Polonia.

was simply accepted as part of being from Polonia. "You knew you had to be at the pilgrimage; you wouldn't think of making other plans for the day."

Keeping tradition alive has always been an important facet of life in the valley. The care lavished on church grounds and buildings is evidence of this and speaks of a loving community that treasures and honours its past. Here, and at the peaceful cemetery overlooking the valley, etched granite cairns and monuments pay tribute to Polonia's pioneers.

The earliest settlers represented a mix of nationalities that were at the time under Austro-Hungarian rule: Poles, Ukrainians, Slovaks, Czechs, and Hungarians. When they came to the valley, de Dory, like the true leader he was, stayed and worked with them until his own untimely death ten years later. Although there were some setbacks with other colonies under the project, this one seemed destined to thrive from the beginning. In the fall of 1887, de Dory wrote, "…my people whom I settled near Minnedosa (Hun's Valley) are all from the first to the last one in every way very contented…."

This fortunate state of affairs was due in part to an assistance scheme arranged with the Manitoba and North Western Railway. According to William R. Smith's *Along the Hills to the Valley* (a history of Hun's Valley – Polonia District 1885-1985), the railway provided the first group of settlers with cattle and a few farm implements to get started. By late that year, seven snug houses had been built of logs and plastered with clay. The 17 families shared these homes for the winter.

The MNWR also offered the men winter jobs cutting cordwood at the edge of the Riding Mountains. Through determination and hard work – toiling on the land in summer, working in the woods in winter – they managed, within six years, to repay most of the loans given them by the railway company.

By 1886, a village site had been surveyed and plans made for a church and school. In 1891 the number of homesteads rose to thirty with more to follow.

The first Hun's Valley School was built in 1887. Classes were conducted in English in compliance with school board rules, but after four o'clock they were offered in Polish. When a replacement school was built in 1911 there were even night classes for adults during the winter.

John Pazdor, a forward-looking pioneer, taught at the school for several years and did much to better the education of Poles in Manitoba, including authoring a book intended to help immigrants learn English. Of a similar mindset, Anthony Prawdzik, local postmaster and school trustee, started a Polish book club from his home and regularly read aloud to those settlers who could not read for themselves.

By now, the Polish influence was very strong in the community. The organizers of the colonization project, themselves Hungarian, had been responsible for naming the area, 'Hun's Valley.' But as time went on and the population became almost entirely Polish, the name was regarded as no longer appropriate.

As well, its connotation changed during the First World War when the Germans were dubbed with the derogatory title, 'Hun', after a race of people (not Hungarians) who long ago had overrun Europe. As a result, the people in the valley chose to call their home Polonia, which is Latin for Poland, and their choice was officially recognized in 1921.

St. Elizabeth's Church, however, retained the name of its Hungarian saint. The first Slavic church in Manitoba, it was originally built in 1887 at the cemetery site. The church at the village location was built to replace it in 1902.

The village of Polonia, though, never did grow much in size. There was a post office but often it was located at the home of whoever held the job of post-master. Stores, too, sometimes developed in the homes of farmers who started out just keeping a few things on

…THE PEOPLE IN THE VALLEY CHOSE TO CALL THEIR HOME POLONIA, WHICH IS LATIN FOR POLAND, AND THEIR CHOICE WAS OFFICIALLY RECOGNIZED IN 1921.

Below: School children of Hun's Valley School in 1904.

Above: The bell stand of St. Elizabeth's Church frames a piece of Polonia history – Don Smith's long-abandoned store.

hand. A blurb for one such venture read, "Our store has now got in a fresh supply of groceries for the spring. You can get anything there from a door lock to a boot lace."

But for a short while there were at least three stores in or close to the village. Joe Terlecki opened a general store in 1927 that became a popular gathering place. He even added a dance hall at the back where patrons sometimes circulated bottles of homebrew for 25 cents each. Movies in the dance hall became part of the attraction in later years. The store operated under various owners until 1962.

Another store, built by Mike Jacynick in 1934, was not so fortunate. It was destroyed by fire after a new owner renovated it into a hall. On the same location near the church, Joe Ostrowski built yet another store, which he ran until 1944. But it, too, succumbed to flames after a change in ownership.

Don Smith's store, built in 1941, was another popular meeting place where families dropped in for treats after church on Sunday. Williams remembers that she and her siblings used to receive fifty cents on Sundays, "Twenty-five cents for the collection plate and twenty-five cents (a gold mine!) to spend at the store."

The men played cards there at night, sometimes until the wee hours of the morning. Tobacco for rolling cigarettes was the most sought after item, according to Don Smith's account in *Along the Hills to the Valley*.

Smith also reminisces about vinegar in wooden kegs, shipments of herring in wooden barrels, and coal oil for lamps. "Heat for the building was supplied by a wood box heater in the middle of the floor," he notes. "On a cold morning it sure didn't take long for the place to warm up."

The hardships of farm life were lightened by get-togethers within the community. Settlers danced in one another's homes and enjoyed games, taffy pulls, box socials, and picnics with horse racing, dancing and baseball. There were concerts at the school, and three-day wedding celebrations besides. One settler, who acquired

a phonograph about 1897, delighted his neighbours by taking it around to community gatherings and playing a selection of music as part of the entertainment. Others contributed songs or recitations, or played the violin and other musical instruments brought from the old country.

Children entered into many of these events and also developed their own pastimes, which included hockey on the slough in winter or tobogganing on the long hill by the school. In time, clubs such as the Catholic Youth Organization and 4H, helped deepen youthful spirituality, round out school education and develop life skills.

But, as a village, Polonia's days were numbered. Young people went away for schooling and jobs and most did not come back to live in the valley. The railroad had never built even a spur-line into the isolated valley, which might have increased growth in the early years. After World War II, with better roads and vehicles, it was easier to go to shop and then to live in other, larger centres. Gradually, farm homes were abandoned.

Joe Miscavish, a lifelong resident, recalls when 17 families lived along a certain stretch of road. "Now there's not a one there," he says. "Only the odd gopher or mole."

Miscavish attended Polonia School when it was at the west approach to the village. "Now it's part of the TIC (Parts and Service) at Neepawa," he notes. The rectory was moved out, too, when there was no longer a resident priest. Some buildings burned down and only a few occupied homes remain in the valley. But even at that, all the land is still farmed. "There is a Hutterite Colony nearby and a few Mennonite families too," Miscavish explains.

Times have changed for Polonia but the beauty of its landscape and the strength of its community endures, as does its church. Together they provide an unbroken link to the past and a continuing source of faith and inspiration for a new age.

ACCESS TO RAILWAYS AND A MEANS OF SUPPORT WERE two factors crucial to the success of pioneer settlements. For these reasons many communities, especially those promoted by greedy entrepreneurs, usually were doomed from birth. But at least one died because of an oversight – an obvious one at that.

In 1907, with the arrival of the Grand Trunk Railway, the townsite of Rea was laid out near the Assiniboine Valley. Its 40 acres included an area large enough for a divisional point to service the pusher engines needed to assist freight trains up the long hill out of the valley. When surveying was completed and development about to start an interesting discovery was made. There was no water.

Since a townsite without water was an obvious handicap, it attracted nobody. The divisional point was moved about 56 km (35 miles) east, and in keeping with the Grand Trunk's custom of alphabetical naming of stations, they called the new station Rivers.

But because the nearby towns of Isabella, Decker and Beulah were still without rail service, the Atlas Grain Company constructed an elevator at Rea to serve them. Rea was also a flag station for freights and a daily passenger train, its buildings consisting of a section house, bunk house and a remodelled box car used for a telegraph station. By 1910, however, these services were no longer needed and the buildings were torn down or moved away.

Eventually even the rails were taken up and all traces of the town disappeared. Rea does retain one distinction – it is probably the only town that failed because its promoters attempted to establish it on land as dry as a hot summer day.

Left: An early barn raising.

SIOUX VILLAGE

SIOUX VILLAGE WAS ESTABLISHED IN 1893 along the Assiniboine River on the southeastern outskirts of Portage la Prairie. The Sioux, or Dakota, who settled there were remnants of the powerful Santee nation (a division of Dakota) dispersed by United States troops following the so-called Minnesota Massacre of 1862 when hundreds of white settlers – men, women and children – were slaughtered.

In late December 1862 and in 1863, with hundreds of their kinsmen, they fled from the United States into the British Northwest expecting the protection of the "Great Mother" (Queen Victoria). They believed that she would honour the memory of Santee allegiance during the war of 1812 and acknowledge their prior residency in the land now under her flag. With them they carried King George III medals which had been given to their forefathers and they told stories of a cannon captured by Dakota warriors and presented to the British during England's long-ago war with the States.

Author Dee Brown's *Bury My Heart At Wounded Knee* describes the appearance at Fort Garry in the spring of 1863 of Little Crow, chief of the Mdewakantons (a subdivision of the Santee) and leader in the uprising: "For his first meeting with them he dressed in his best clothing – a black coat with a velvet collar, a blue breechcloth and deerskin leggings."

Before the outbreak, Little Crow had farmed, lived in a house and attended the Episcopal Church. He reminded the British of their promise to return the captured cannon to the Dakota and give them men to work it if ever they were in trouble. The Minnesota outbreak, he maintained, was the result of years of oppression and harassment from the "long knives" (Americans) who wished to take over Aboriginal lands but would not pay for them as promised.

Annual treaty payments due to the Dakota in June 1862 had, in fact, not been made and the traders immediately withdrew credit, cutting off the Aboriginals' source of food. One trader, Andrew Myrick, was heartless enough to tell the hungry Sioux to "eat grass." He was one of the first killed in the uprising and his body was later found with his mouth stuffed with grass. In a message to American General Sibley during the hostilities, Little Crow pointed out the traders' callousness as one of the reasons for the war.

According to Rev. G. Laviolette OMI, author of *The Sioux Indians in Canada*, the Dakota saw themselves engaged, not in massacre, but in war, "...the most

Opposite: The old Hudson's Bay Company post at Portage la Prairie in 1890.

honourable of all pursuits, against men who robbed them of their country and their freedom."

But they were not received as heroes at Fort Garry in the Red River Settlement. At best they were tolerated, given gifts of food and urged to return to the United States. At worst, an official blind eye was turned when two Dakota chiefs, Little Six (half-brother to Little Crow) and Medicine Bottle, were abducted from Fort Garry by an American lieutenant, in contravention of international law, and later hanged. Other refugees were reviled or ignored. Some were even attacked by bands of Saulteaux.

Supplies were scarce at Red River in the winter of 1863-1864. It had been a poor crop year and the fall buffalo hunt was a failure. Local Aboriginals and Metis jealously guarded what little they had and the white settlers were uneasy. The Dakota were reduced to begging in the streets, their clothes in tatters.

"One could see the men wandering about the settlement with a gaunt skeletal look, and imploring help with hoarse voices," wrote Father Laviolette. "Driving them away in that pitiable state would have been tantamount to murder."

Governor Dallas of the Hudson's Bay Company issued some supplies to the destitute Sioux and nervous settlers aided them substantially as well. Soon, of their own accord, they began to move westward, distributing themselves in camps along the Assiniboine River at Sturgeon Creek, White Horse Plain, Poplar Point, High Bluff and Portage la Prairie.

In *An Economic History of the Dakota in Canada,* Peter Douglas Elias, Ph.D., explains: "Initially they had gone to the Red River for safety, provisions, and a little breathing space, but as soon as was possible, they began to make their peace with their neighbours and re-establish their shattered lives."

By the mid 1860s, Elias notes, this peace seems to have been attained, the final act of violence against the Dakota taking place in the summer of 1866. This outbreak happened near Portage la Prairie where Red Lake Ojibway attacked a small band of Dakota, killing the chief and his son.

By 1869 there were nearly 500 Dakota camped in the vicinity of Portage la Prairie alone but it wasn't until 1873 that their presence in Canada was officially accepted. In April of that year an Order-in-Council approved by the Earl of Dufferin, Governor-General of Canada, authorized the Sioux immigrants "continuance under the British Flag." Earlier in the same year the governor-general had approved the appropriation of land for the establishment of Dakota reserves. The reserves were granted, however, as "a matter of grace and not a matter

THE DAKOTA
WERE REDUCED
TO BEGGING IN
THE STREETS,
THEIR CLOTHES
IN TATTERS.

Below: Sioux encampment on the prairie.

of right." The reason was that the Dakota, in spite of their claims, were considered by authorities to be American Aboriginals with no land rights in Canada.

In any event, it took more than ten years for the policy to be fully implemented and even then, not all Dakota were inclined to accept the favour. At Portage la Prairie "one small group numbering twenty-three families in 1886 (preferring not to move to a reserve) remained in the vicinity of the old settlement." They fished Lake Manitoba, hunted, trapped, cut wood and hay and hired out as labourers to local settlers and townspeople. In this way they earned their livelihood and began to accumulate the funds with which they would purchase their own land.

The river-lots where they were camped in tents were privately owned and not for sale, but in 1893 the Dakota arranged to buy 25 acres on nearby Lot 99. Here they began to build their homes.

The first houses were made of logs with sod roofs and floors of hard-packed earth. By the turn of the cen-tury, however, the village was described as "a model of its kind" with a straight street, whitewashed homes with shingled roofs, clean and comfortably furnished, and splendid gardens of vegetables and flowers. A Presbyterian church was built and the children attended school in Portage la Prairie. Many of the young women earned good salaries as domestics in town.

In spite of their close association with white socie-ty, the Dakota managed to keep alive their ancient customs even though some religious ceremonies like the Sun Dance were prohibited. The rich cultural and spiritual heritage of the Dakota was overlooked, though, by many Portage la Prairie pioneers. They saw the Dakota as simple pagans "…roaming about our streets in paint and feathers with no thought of God except in a dim idea of a great spirit…" Nevertheless, relations between the townspeople and the villagers were gener-ally good. Dakota labourers were in demand and the village might have continued to prosper except for several converging factors.

THE FIRST HOUSES WERE MADE OF LOGS WITH SOD ROOFS AND FLOORS OF HARD-PACKED EARTH.

In 1902 and again in 1905 the Assiniboine River flooded, carrying off several village houses. Although the Dakota rebuilt their homes, the river gradually began to wear away the land on which the village stood. Overcrowding became a problem by 1906 when the population reached 125. Then in 1911 a resolution by Portage la Prairie City Council recommended that the villagers be removed from their present location: "It would be advisable to have them placed where they would have more land for farm purposes."

The Dakota themselves had been trying unsuccessfully to acquire land adjacent to their village and found the alternatives now presented to them unsatisfactory. A move to Bird Tail or Oak Lake Reserves, 200 km (120 miles) to the west, would mean selling Lot 99 and their homes of twenty years. Further, it would mean leaving well-paying jobs and the way of life which they had developed on their own land.

The matter dragged on for several years. Some families did relocate, reducing the population of Sioux Village to only sixty by 1924. By this time postwar depression had cut wages in half and many of the Dakota lost their jobs to the incoming unemployed from Eastern Canada.

The crisis was eased somewhat when William E. Ronald built an icehouse in Portage la Prairie about 1928 and hired several Dakota to cut river-ice at the village. Mike Chiponski of Portage la Prairie who later owned and operated the business was an employee of

Above: The Dakota camped on the river-lots until they accumulated funds to buy their own land. They fished, hunted, trapped, cut wood and hired out as labourers.

Ronald in the early years. He remembered the villagers as "hard workers who did all the ice cutting.

"They used to gouge the line with a type of walking plow with a narrow blade and one of the boys earned ten cents a day for leading the horse. All day he would lead the horse up and down the ice and the men would come along behind with saw. They got a dollar a day for cutting and hauling." It was cold, gruelling work, especially when the Assiniboine froze to a depth of 38 inches but the wages were considered good for the times. Sadly, they were not good enough to halt the decline of the village.

By 1933 several more families had moved to reserve land adjacent to Long Plains Saulteaux Reserve 25 km (15 miles) west of Portage la Prairie, leaving only 28 people at the village. Meanwhile, portions of Lot 99 continued to disappear into the Assiniboine River.

Nevertheless, more than two decades were to pass before a severe flood in 1955 forced a decision. The Dakota villagers, by this time numbering 86, accepted the inevitable and agreed to move to the western outskirts of Portage la Prairie to land now known as Dakota Tipi First Nation Reserve. In 1957 the move was complete. The abandoned property was partially used for dyking the Assiniboine River and the balance sold for $1,900, proceeds to be reserved for a community centre at the new location.

It is not known whether the community centre actually was built with these funds. In any case, the memory of Sioux Village and its people lives on in another special way. On a gentle slope near the old village site, the Dakota had for many years buried their dead. Owner of the land Guthrie Paterson, a local farmer, continued to allow access to the little cemetery and in 1959 arranged with the Manitoba Historical Society to erect a cairn with a bronze plaque commemorating those who had died since 1871. Here, in the midst of a modern grain field, the old Dakota names evoke visions of a distant past.

SOURIS CITY

STORIES OF THE EARLY SETTLEMENTS OFTEN REVOLVE around the stamina and enterprise of one or two outstanding individuals or families. Souris City, a village which was 40 km (25 miles) southeast of Brandon, is a typical example.

In 1879 a group of men including Dick Cory, his two sons, Gus and Richard, and Thomas and Orlin Elliott (no relation) journeyed west to find land. On their way they stopped at High Bluff, near Portage la Prairie, long enough to sow a crop of oats. Then they continued west to the beautiful Brandon Hills and Souris River. Alongside a stream, which Dick Cory named Black Creek, they staked homesteads. After cutting a winter's supply of hay, the Corys and Orlin Elliott returned to High Bluff to harvest the oats.

When they returned to their Black Creek homestead, they found that prairie fires had destroyed their hay, clothing, machinery and tools. In spite of this dismaying loss, they began work on a sod and log shanty but were so alarmed by packs of prowling timber wolves that they dared not work alone or after dark. This unexpected intrusion slowed the project considerably.

The little group finally settled in for the winter but by the end of February their provisions were reduced to tea and flour. The two older men left for Portage la Prairie, 120 km (75 miles) away, while Gus and Richard Cory stayed to tend the livestock.

The boys nearly perished. The winter was cruel and they managed to snare only one rabbit to relieve their monotonous diet of tea and bannock. The oxen starved to death and the Corys, without proper tools and half-starved themselves, lacked the energy to butcher the frozen carcasses for food. It was two months before a group of about twenty settlers, led by three Elliott brothers, arrived to save the boys from death by starvation.

This group formed the beginning of the Elliott settlement (forerunner of Souris City) and it quickly prospered. In 1882 the Manitoba Daily Free Press reported: "The Elliott family, who are the pioneers of this, the best stretch of land we have yet seen, deserve the greatest confidence and regard of the settlement they have worked so hard to establish. When we drove past their splendid fields of grain, and past their comfortable homes, and saw what

Centre: As the Cory boys learned in the bitter winter of 1880 when they almost died of starvation, during the pioneer era youths had to do the work of men. An example is the young man stooking near Makinak in the early 1900s.

improvements had been made…we could only compare them to the happy Arcadians so graphically described by Longfellow in Evangeline."

One of the most popular pastimes of the settlers who preceded the railways was speculating where the rails would be laid. Since the exact routes were seldom divulged until the railway companies had picked the potential townsites, settlers and promoters had to guess the route. Although chances of predicting the correct route were poor, promoters gambled with gusto. After all, the money they used was seldom their own.

The Souris City gamblers were William Scott and his son, William J. Scott, who arrived in 1880. They had been contractors in Toronto and immediately began buying land and arranging with the CPR for more. A year later they had a townsite surveyed and the plan registered. Shortly after, they sold all their land, including the townsite, to the Manitoba and Nor'West Company Ltd., a company in which Scott Sr. was a promoter. By the spring of 1882 the town was well underway.

That August the *Manitoba Daily Free Press* noted: "From Langvale the trail runs over the Tiger Hills to the crossing of the Souris at Souris City, which we found to have made a considerable start towards a metropolis. Mr. Scott, the energetic founder of the town, is one of the solid men of this section of the country and his liberal policy of granting free sites to all who wish to build in Souris City is sure to bring a good class of settler to this already rich and well settled district."

By this time Souris City had a gristmill as well as two stores, a hotel, blacksmith shop and a school. It also had a problem. Like a bigamist, the name of the post office changed with bewildering frequency. First called Sourisbourg, it then became Wawonaissa, then

Below: Sod buildings like this one provided snug shelter for many during settlement days.

Sourisbourg again. Finally, to the relief of local residents who by now were not sure where they lived, in 1884 it became what it should have been at the start – Souris City.

Another unsettling problem was a bridge. In 1882 a 96-metre (320-foot) structure costing $9,000 was built over the Souris River. Sadly, the night before it was to be dedicated – indeed, during the time that the provincial dignitary who was to perform the honour was quenching his thirst with some of the locals – an ice-packed spring freshet ripped out a good portion.

The bridge was repaired with the added precaution of centre spans designed so that they could be removed during spring break-up, something like a giant Meccano set. This modification proved expensive and the municipal council resented having to pay the entire maintenance costs even though municipalities to the south also used it. In 1889 they rid themselves of the burden by having the bridge dismantled.

The year before they had solved another transportation problem in the same forthright manner. This

IN 1882 A 96-METRE (320-FOOT) STRUCTURE COSTING $9,000 WAS BUILT OVER THE SOURIS RIVER.

problem was that the CPR had an agreement with Sir John A. Macdonald's federal Conservative government that no rival branch lines could be built in a southerly direction from their main line for twenty-five years. This clause caused resentment among the settlers since they had to haul their grain 40 km (25 miles) to Brandon. Settlers in other areas were equally unhappy and in the 1888 provincial election the Conservatives were tossed

Above: Red River carts at Portage la Prairie in 1880. From Souris City settlers at first travelled 120 km (75 miles) to Portage la Prairie by horses or oxen for supplies.

out. The incoming Liberals, under Thomas Greenway, broke the CPR's monopoly clause.

To celebrate, the people of Souris City held a huge picnic. "Goodbye Monopoly" and "Railway Competition Has Come" were signs greeting the 2,000 or so people who attended, with new Premier Greenway the guest of honour. He was welcomed by former reeve James Hector who said: "The people of Souris City district most heartily join in extending to you a very cordial welcome on this occasion. Your presence, and that of your colleagues, with us today, enhances very greatly the gratification we all experience in celebrating the advent in our midst of the Northern Pacific and Manitoba Railway."

As jubilant Souris City residents applauded the speakers they little realized that they were hearing their own funeral oration. When the anticipated Morris branch line was completed the following year, it crossed the river about five km (three miles) downstream where a new community called Wawanesa was born.

Souris City was doomed. Today nothing remains to indicate where the Scotts lost their gamble with both railways and politics.

SPEARHILL

ALTHOUGH MANY EARLY TOWNS and settlements were abandoned because the proposed railway missed them, Spearhill's demise as a town, occurred for an entirely different reason. The town moved away from its only industry and not the other way around.

In 1911, the family of Sven Carlson arrived from Norway and settled in the area about five miles east of Moosehorn village. They lived in tents and a cave until they could cut wood for houses. A small 'pot' kiln was also built to burn enough limestone to use for white-washing and plastering their cabins.

The beginning of large scale limestone quarrying, however, had to wait three or four years until after the Canadian National Railway built a spur line from Moosehorn to the site which was located on a limestone ridge. Here, the Moosehorn Lime Company began operations.

Since many settlers on the surrounding farms found the land to be unproductive, they were glad to find employment with the company. These workers, who occupied shacks and tents known as 'the camp', built the kilns, barns, and a boarding house. To serve their needs and others in the area, the manager of the plant, J.R. Spears, also had them erect a building to house a store and post office, which he also operated. Thus began the town of Spearhill, named in honor of its founder.

When, in 1919, Winnipeg Supply and Fuel pur-chased the quarry company from the original owners, output was increased and about fifty men were employed. Other hiring had to be done to facilitate the operation. Stablemen were needed to tend the horses, which were used for hauling quarry cars. Coopers were required to build the barrels in which the lime was shipped and several rows of long, low buildings built near the kilns were used for drying and seasoning the staves.

Since the kilns used wood to burn the stone, more horses and men were needed to keep up the fuel supply. Sometimes there were over 80 teams of horses hauling wood to Spearhill. In a 1980 interview with Lillian (Mrs.Lawrence) Cook, she recalled that although her father, Mr. Redwood, had a farm, he also worked as a teamster at the quarry site using his own horses. He stayed in town during the week while the rest of the family remained on the farm.

A hall was built with volunteer labour and Mrs. Cook said that on Friday nights, her mother and the children often drove the 10 miles into town to attend dances where Mrs. Redwood provided the piano music. "We'd come in by horse and buggy, through all those sloughs. Sometimes, she played for five hours straight. Square dances and everything. I don't know how she

SINCE THE KILNS USED WOOD TO BURN THE STONE, MORE HORSES AND MEN WERE NEEDED TO KEEP UP THE FUEL SUPPLY.

ever did it. For this, they gave her five dollars – big money in those days." In 1927, when Mr. Redwood gave up farming and moved his family into town, he stayed on at the plant.

The school, called Scandia, built by the original Norwegian settlers, rapidly filled with students as the town grew. Teachers were required to teach grades one through eight. Grades nine and ten could be acquired through correspondence courses, but for further education, students had to travel to other towns. Val (Francis) Campbell's father owned the store and she attended Scandia school. Mrs. Campbell recalls, "I think most of our teachers tried to contribute to extra-curricular activities, but were limited by lack of funds. However, we played lots of games such as baseball, football and prisoner's base. Whatever game we played had to include children of all ages."

Above: Limestone cliffs at Spearhill.

Churches, too, were needed and, although services were held in homes for the most part, the Lutherans did build a church, which sported a box heater. Unfortunately, the first time the heater was used, it overheated and burned the building to the ground. Later, a United Church congregation met in the school and then in the community hall. Some members, though, deemed it unseemly to use the hall for church services when it was also being used for dances. So, because the unused Blair school was available, it was decided to move it to town to be used by any Christian denomination. By dint of great effort over a period of a year, it was finally maneuvered over boggy terrain the five miles south to its new location in Spearhill.

Cordwood hauling provided extra income to area farmers and, because the plant and the store worked in conjunction, the wood was delivered to the store and exchanged for groceries and other necessities. Cash seldom changed hands. The store, always known as Schofield's General Store and Post Office, was owned and managed by Dick Francis from 1926 to 1966. Until

1950, it boasted the only telephone in town as well as providing just about everything else a family could need – from cosmetics to hardware and from drugs to a news stand and fur exchange. They also sold gas, oil and coal.

Wood hauling, however, grew expensive and problematic when trees became scarcer and more distant. Therefore, in 1929, a new kiln was added and the original three were remodeled to accommodate the burning of bituminous coal, which produced the gas needed to fire the kilns. This alteration brought changes in personnel, as well, and other tradesmen such as engineers, steel workers and electricians moved in. To house them, a second boarding house was built which employed a housekeeper and cook.

Over the years more homes were built for workers, many of whom had abandoned their land and moved to town. The community hall became a busy place for social functions such as whist drives, box and pie socials, dances etc. (And always, a Robbie Burns Supper for the many Scottish men in the area.) Mrs. Cook thought back fondly to the excellent Christmas Concerts. "I remember my mother spending hours and hours making angel dresses, and the like, then playing the piano for the occasion."

Although the town never had a curling rink, there was a good skating rink for winter sports and Lillian Cook spoke of other childhood activities: "Now and again, we used to load up the old push car with kids and away we went to Moosehorn. That was fine, but it wasn't so much fun coming home because it was all up hill and nobody wanted to push – especially if we were tired from playing ball all day in Moosehorn. But we did it, anyhow." Apparently, adults looked the other way during these adventures and no harm was done. "I guess we weren't supposed to use the push car, but we always put it back where we got it. Took it off the track, so it didn't interfere with the train or anything."

There were hazards connected with living so close to the mining operation. Mrs. Cook spoke of blasting explosions in the quarry and the resultant tremors in the residential area during which dishes rattled in cupboards. In the beginning there was no warning, but later, a siren was sounded around town alerting residents to the impending explosions. Occasionally, flying rocks added to the excitement and she clearly recalls a stone hurtling through a window and another penetrating their large rain barrel. Although odors from cordite used in explosives as well as from the burning lime often hung in the air, they were not offensive. Or, perhaps, residents simply got used to them.

Speaking of Spearhill, a book compiled by L. Jean Jardine, provides the following information about the town's industry. Lime is made from the burning of limestone. The rock is loaded into a kiln, which is heated to 1050 degrees Centigrade. It then decomposes into 'quick lime' (CaO) as it moves downward. During the final four-hour process, while in the hottest zone, it is converted completely to lime. A typical kiln production might be 50 to 60 tons per day.

Lime, the cheapest alkali, has many uses. It is used in sugar production, brick, glass and cement making, petroleum refining, water softening, sewage purification, agriculture and in a myriad of other ways.

Spearhill lime, almost pure calcium lime, was used mainly in the manufacture of sugar, flux in steel making, calcium in stock foods, poultry grit and railway ballast. However, it 'slakes' very rapidly when moistened and causes burning to anyone in contact with it – particularly the men who were employed in crushing and bagging. Problems occurred more commonly during the heat of the summer when men perspired heavily. Workers wore masks to prevent damage to their lungs and nasal membranes and Mrs. Cook remembered seeing a neighbor wearing a protective wrapping around his neck as well. The slaking was often a shipping problem, too, as the lime would slake off from moisture in the air, become overheated and cause fires in the box cars.

The backbreaking process of limestone quarrying involved sorting and loading the rock into quarry cars to be taken to the kilns. This was accomplished by hardy

Above: Remains of village at Spearhill.

workers using sledge hammers, rock chisels and picks and shovels. They were paid by the carload and the rock ranged in value from the smallest size (termed 'fine sugar') which brought the most money. The scale dropped accordingly as the size grew larger – 'sugar' then 'kiln stone', then 'rubble', with 'dirt' being the least valuable. The latter, not burned, was sold as raw stone.

Eventually, mechanization, which also increased output, decreased the numbers of men required. The chief reason for the demise of the village, however, was the relocation of the homes. They were situated on top of a considerable amount of good limestone, which the company wished to mine. Because increased mobility no longer required workers to live at their place of employment, the company offered the residences for sale to employees with the stipulation that they be removed from the site. With the houses moved to places such as Moosehorn and Ashern, there was no longer a need for the school or a store and post office and the end came when Dick Francis closed Schofield's Ltd. in 1966 and moved to Winnipeg.

SPEARHILL LIME, ALMOST PURE CALCIUM LIME, WAS USED MAINLY IN THE MANUFACTURE OF SUGAR, FLUX IN STEEL MAKING, CALCIUM IN STOCK FOODS, POULTRY GRIT AND RAILWAY BALLAST.

STE. ELIZABETH

A YOUNG PRIEST FROM QUEBEC WHO DREAMED OF ATTRACTING French-Canadian settlers to the Red River Valley is credited with founding four French-Canadian parishes here, one of them the parish (and village) of Ste. Elizabeth (sometimes spelled in the French way as Ste. Elisabeth). Reverend Father David Fillion was born at St. Hermas, P. Q. in 1845, ordained a priest in 1870 and came to the Red River Valley as a missionary in 1873.

His superior, Bishop A. A. Taché, not only shared his dream but in 1874 formed the Manitoba Society for Colonization. He subsequently gave Father Fillion permission to travel to the industrial cities of New England in company with a federal land agent. Once there, the young priest met with families who had left Quebec to find work in the mills, persuading them that the Red River Valley offered them a better life.

Over the next few decades French-Canadian settlers moved onto the fertile plains south of Winnipeg along the Red River and its tributaries. They joined pioneers of various nationalities already homesteading there. Sometimes it happened that a French-Canadian living in the United States lost his French language and had to re-learn it when he moved to the Red River. One former resident recalls that this happened to her great-grandfather so that ever after he spoke French with an English accent and a bit of a drawl.

As more and more French-Canadians arrived from the United States and from the Province of Quebec, interest in establishing a parish church in the region of the Marsh River grew. In 1898, when Father Adélard Fournier celebrated Mass in the home of Mr. and Mrs. Adolphe Lacharité, the event became generally regarded as the beginnings of Ste. Elizabeth. It wasn't until 1901, however, that Father J.M. Jolys, parish priest of St. Pierre, officially founded the parish of Ste. Elizabeth.

Father Elie Rocan was named pastor of the new parish and a rectory was built with an upstairs chapel. In the same year, according to Claire Désharnais in *Reapers of the Valley 1882-1982* (published by the Montcalm History Group) plans were made for a barn-like building that became the parish hall. Parishioners donated five dollars each towards its construction. When Bishop Langevin came the following year for his first pastoral visit, he bestowed the sacrament of confirmation upon 29 parishioners and also blessed the steel church bell.

The bishop's visits were always celebrated with special ceremony. Parishioners went out to meet him, accompanying him on foot or by horse and wagon to the village. Meanwhile the church bell was rung continuously until his arrival – except for the time the

Opposite: Once the storekeeper's home, this abandoned building still stands in Ste. Elizabeth.

rope broke and the bell-ringer had to clamber into the steeple to start it pealing again.

The first church building was started in the summer of 1903. Measuring 60 by 40 feet, it cost more than $3,500. By 1905, the interior and steeple were not yet finished and in fact it took eight more years before work on the steeple could be considered complete. The results must have been worth the wait though, as former residents still remark on the beauty of that first church.

Parishioners drove in from farms within a radius of five to ten miles to attend Mass on Sunday mornings. Afterwards, they enjoyed a visit with neighbours in the churchyard, at village homes or even in one of the stores, where the children could look forward to a treat of ice cream.

Christmas Eve services ushered in a special round of visiting and celebration for the French-Canadian families that continued for twelve days until Epiphany. After midnight Mass they gathered with friends and family for Réveillon, a time of feasting, especially on tourtière (meat pie) and ragoût de pattes (stewed pig's feet). There

would be lots of singing and jigging to the music of the fiddle or someone playing the spoons. Children opened their gifts or fell asleep until the party broke up at dawn. On New Year's Day, the extended family gathered to kneel before father or grandfather to receive the paternal blessing. This was an ingrained and much revered tradition, some married sons rising as early as five or six a.m. in order to pay such respect to their elders.

Hockey games in winter and baseball in the summer provided further opportunity for socializing. Women and children came out to support the teams and more than one marriage in the community resulted from a chance meeting at a ball game. The Ste. Elizabeth baseball team of early days garnered fame, if not fortune, as they scooped up numerous 'firsts' in community tournaments and across the border in North Dakota. Former resident, Léa (Rivard) Guénette, whose father was a member of the award-winning team, recalled how dedicated he was to the game. "After spending a long day working in the fields with the draft horses he knew the animals were exhausted," she said. "So he left them at home to rest while he walked the two and a half miles into town to play baseball!''

Other outlets for sociability over the years were a community hall on the second floor of a vacated store and, of course, the various stores themselves. The first general store in town, operated by Henri Fontaine, opened in 1901. Not only did it carry a variety of goods for the fledgling community, it also housed the post office, a boarding place, and a barber shop and pool room that became a gathering place for young and old.

Two brothers, Odilon and Josephat Desaulniers later purchased the Fontaine store. They built a new one in 1923 and the old store eventually became a cheese factory for about six years. The Desaulniers operated the new store until 1937 when the Great Depression was taking its grim toll on both farming and business.

A number of French settlers who came to the Ste. Elizabeth area about 1911 bought their farmland from one of the land agencies in the area, some of which were backed by huge financial interests in the United States. In the 1920s, one of the companies actually flew prospective clients to view the land. The H. L. Emmert Land Agency, the American Land Company, and the Rohrer and Sheppard Ranch all owned extensive tracts of land in Manitoba and at least one of them operated a hog and cattle business, employing dozens of men. Fortunately for those who followed, they had also made a good beginning on road building and drainage canals.

In March 1925 the first six Mennonite families arrived in the Ste. Elizabeth area from Russia, to be followed by another seventeen families by April 1926. At first they met in one another's homes for Sunday worship services but soon acquired a small building near Ste. Elizabeth School to use as a church.

Their relationship with the townsfolk was pleasant and mutually beneficial. They took their cream to Desaulniers' store for delivery to Morris and brought eggs to trade for items they needed. To facilitate such transactions with the French-Canadian proprietor, the resourceful German-speaking women underlined needed items in their German-English dictionary. He in turn encouraged them in their language lessons.

Of Days Gone By, a history of Ste. Elizabeth district, provides a pioneer woman's view of one of the town's blacksmiths. She found him always obliging as he shod their horses, sharpened their plowshares, and tightened the iron rims on their wagon wheels, which tended to dry out and shrink in the summer heat.

Although Ste. Elizabeth never became very large, there were at least fifteen family homes in the village and several businesses in addition to the stores and cheese factory. Former residents mention the Bank of Hochelaga, which operated across from the church and the Credit Union, which, in 1939, opened in its own premises. There was a livery stable, a restaurant and during one period, even a milliner. The Desaulniers ran a

Below: Farm families drove for miles around to patronize Ste. Elizabeth's stores and businesses, and on Sundays they drove in to attend church.

transfer business in connection with their store and, beginning in 1946, a garage catered to the owners of automobiles and other vehicles until newly accessible towns and cities drained away its clientele.

But perhaps one of the most appreciated services of all was that supplied by the local midwife. Delphine (Duprey) Rivard was born in Massachusetts in 1871 to parents from Quebec. Following her marriage in 1888 to Jean-Baptiste Rivard and the birth of their first two children in North Dakota, the young couple relocated in 1902 to a homestead near Ste. Elizabeth. Here, while her husband farmed, Delphine tended her growing family, her bee-hives, and a large garden; sold butter and eggs and sewed quilts, rugs and even wedding dresses when the time came. She also kept boarders and cared for foster children.

Delphine's great-granddaughter, Pauline (Guénette) Chudzik remembers her as "a quiet, unassuming pioneer woman." Yet, no matter how severe the weather or how bad the situation, this remarkable mother of eleven set out from her home to give help where it was needed. She helped bring more than two hundred babies into the world.

"When the doctor called with news of a woman in labour, Delphine would head out immediately," Chudzik said in an interview. "Often she would assist at the birth before the doctor arrived."

Many times Delphine stayed on to care for the mother, baby and family. "She would be gone for a week or more," said Chudzik. "Olivine, the youngest girl at home remembers those times well because she was left to cook and clean for her father and the others."

In 1940, after nearly forty years on the farm, Delphine and Jean-Baptiste Rivard retired to the village of Ste. Elizabeth, where Delphine continued her community work.

In 1950 the village had to deal with the devastating Red River flood which took the life of one resident who tried to cross the Marsh River in a canoe. The following year parishioners received another blow when fire destroyed Ste. Elizabeth's Church and rectory. They immediately began to build a new church out of concrete blocks. A hired contractor with volunteer labour and financial aid from neighbouring districts helped bring about the completion of the church in 1952.

But business in Ste. Elizabeth gradually declined for reasons already familiar to similar prairie towns. Drought and depression, war and flood, improved roads and better vehicles allowing access to larger centres, consolidation of schools, larger farms and the need for the young to find jobs elsewhere all contributed to Ste. Elizabeth's demise.

Stores and businesses closed. By 1970 only two families still lived in the once vibrant village. Finally, after years without a resident priest, even the church was sold.

About 1979 in what seemed like a reprieve for the town, a group from Quebec founded a Christian colony at Ste. Elizabeth. Self-described in a *Winnipeg Sun* article as "a lot like the Hutterites," the group of sixteen men, women and children wanted to live in community to support one another and strengthen their Christian faith. They acquired several homes damaged by the flood of 1979 and local farmers donated two other buildings. To help support themselves the group opened a woodworking shop, where they built and repaired furniture. But it didn't last and once again Ste. Elizabeth stood deserted.

Thanks to a group of former residents and friends, however, neither parish nor town will be forgotten. They have formed the Ste. Elizabeth Historical Committee for the preservation of Ste. Elizabeth Church. In an arrangement with the Archdiocese of St. Boniface they were able to buy back the church and are now in the process of restoring it.

Meanwhile, member Yolande Rheault is preparing a history book and the committee plans to establish a small-scale museum in the church.

Above: Reverend Father David Fillion came from Quebec in 1873. He is credited with founding four parishes in the Red River Valley, one of them Ste. Elizabeth.

TOTOGAN

A BOGGY STRIP OF WILLOWS AND TIME-WORN WOODEN PILES are today about all that remains of Totogan, a community its businessmen once touted as another Chicago. Located at the fork of the Whitemud River and Rat Creek (formerly Willow Bend Creek), the site of the community founded so optimistically is now a cultivated field.

The Aboriginal word "totogan" means a "low, swampy place" but if early promoters were aware of this interpretation they paid it scant heed – an oversight they later regretted. Their eyes were on the north – on the vast stretch of forest and the wide waters of Lake Manitoba. Their thoughts were occupied with the opportunities offered by easily accessible timber, fish, and minerals.

In the early 1800s hunters and trappers frequented the area and, according to local lore, the Metis once had a small village with church and burial grounds on the banks of Rat Creek. There was little change until the late 1860s when the first white settlers took up land for farming.

One of those who moved in before the Aboriginals' title to the land was extinguished by treaties was Tom Wallace. A hotel keeper from Portage la Prairie who intended to go into ranching or mixed farming, he set up a tent and began to erect a log house. His claim to the land, like that of other settlers, was a tenuous one based on the custom of squatters' rights which allowed each man to hold the land he occupied and no more. The Aboriginals objected to Wallace's intrusion. Several times they ordered him off the land they considered theirs.

When Wallace continued to ignore them they dismantled the half-finished walls of his cabin, piled his belongings into his pony cart, and firmly invited him to take up the reins and leave. Wallace, in the interests of continuing good health, accepted the invitation. But other settlers, when similarly challenged, plied the Aboriginals with food and promises to pay for the land if the government did not. Such were their powers of persuasion that the tribes left them in peace to develop their farms. By 1872 the Totogan area was attracting increasing attention and publicity.

The *Manitoba Free Press* for December 21, 1872, announced that $1,000 was paid by H.B. Chisholm for a 160 acre tract of land on the Whitemud River "for a mill site." The report added: "We are glad to hear that

Opposite: Robert Campbell refused $40,000 for his townsite of Totogan.

...100 LOTS
WERE SOLD
EARLY IN 1874
"AT PRICES
RANGING FROM
$95 TO $105."

Below: The Lady Blanche and a barge on the Whitemud River in 1893. The vessel built in 1883, was first used to tow spruce logs from Dog Hung Bay on Lake Manitoba to the mill at Totogan.

some of those who first settled in the newer part of the Province are already reaping the advantages of a wise and fortunate selection in the advance of values." Chisholm, with his partner, G. Bubar, built a sawmill, a gristmill, a large hotel and a general store. They also had their land surveyed into city lots.

According to a later *Free Press* report, 100 lots were sold early in 1874 "at prices ranging from $95 to $105." That year, too, Donald Stewart constructed a 61 metre (200 foot) bridge across the Whitemud, the first bridge of notable size west of Winnipeg. It was used for three years during which time it accommodated Red River carts, dog sleighs, and other conveyances heading westward across the prairies some 1,300 km (800 miles) to Fort Edmonton.

Workmen's shacks grew up around the mills and several new businesses, including a blacksmith shop and salt works, were established. Chisholm and Bubar, with characteristic enthusiasm, advertised in the *Free Press*

their intention to "keep constantly on hand Pine Lumber of all dimensions" as well as "SALT from the Salt springs of Lake Winnipegosis, a beautiful article." Similarly, the new blacksmith, A.C. McKay, informed the public of his willingness "to execute, on shortest notice, all manner of work."

In 1876 the Totogan Post Office opened with John C. Ball as postmaster. The Hudson's Bay Company became interested in the town and moved its trading post from Westbourne to Totogan in 1878. Almost everything pointed to prosperous times ahead. Boats and barges negotiated the winding channel of the Whitemud to Totogan, bringing logs, minerals, and fish from Lake Manitoba and further north. They took back lumber, merchandise and passengers.

To capitalize on this trade Chisholm and Bubar built the hull of a vessel intended to be a steam tug. They christened her *Saskatchewan* but she never did steam. For some reason when her hull was completed the engine

ALL THAT REMAINS OF TOTOGAN
ARE A FEW WOODEN PILES FROM
THE GYPSUM COMPANY'S WHARF.

Above: A logging operation in 1883.

had not arrived and she left on her maiden voyage with a sail for power. Although another steamboat, the *Lady Blanche*, was later built at Totogan and operated successfully for years, such was not the fate of the *Saskatchewan*. According to historian Robert B. Hill, a storm during her last trip of the year blew her off course "and beached her in a reedy marsh…a few miles east of her native port." Attempts to get her afloat were unsuccessful and she was destroyed by a prairie fire that swept the region the following year.

In addition to the ever-present danger of prairie fires, another problem was spring flooding. The vital bridge was swept away in 1877 and Chisholm and Bubar's grand enterprise began to show signs of collapse. Funds ran out in 1878, forcing them into liquidation. Chisholm had additional troubles when he refused to surrender the books and was jailed for contempt of court.

New life was infused into the lumber industry when W.M. Smith purchased the sawmill. He was joined in 1879 by W.J.M. Pratt. About this time the townsite was taken over by Robert Campbell, a Scot who had been an explorer in the north and a Hudson's Bay Company Chief Factor. His faith in the community was shared by others and he was offered $40,000 for the townsite. He refused. Then, at his own expense, he even built and furnished a little Presbyterian church. But neither church nor town was destined to survive.

For three successive years from 1881 the level of Lake Manitoba rose. As a consequence, northerly winds drove water over the river banks, flooding some of Totogan's buildings and floating others. It was too much for Pratt and he abandoned the mill. By this time many of the settlers had also decided to leave.

Totogan's business flagged even more as a steamboat builder named McArthur went into the freighting business a few miles upstream. A spur track from the Manitoba and North Western Railway added to the attractiveness of McArthur's location. But there were still people in Totogan who refused to let the community wither. A new townsite was started on the opposite side of the Whitemud River to the south and the Manitoba Gypsum Company built a wharf and other facilities. But this resurrection was doomed when the Canadian Northern Railway completed a line up the east side of Lake Manitoba to Gypsumville, source of the gypsum.

All that remains of Totogan are a few wooden piles from the Gypsum Company's wharf. They stand just below the water line at the river's edge – silent reminders of a vanished dream.

WAKOPA

SOUTHWEST OF KILLARNEY, NOT FAR FROM THE INTERNATIONAL BORDER, lies the little ghost town of Wakopa. Over a century ago, at a slightly different location, it was a bustling new community, the first in the Turtle Mountain district and the most important until the CPR reached Killarney in 1885.

The town grew up on both sides of the Boundary Commission Trail where Bernard B. LaRiviere built a trading post and an inn in 1877. He had scouted the land the previous year and selected a site in the elbow of the Long River where rings of stones from Aboriginal tipis and the ashes of campfires indicated its popularity as a stopping place. No doubt the presence nearby of a supply depot built by the Boundary Commission, who were surveying the Canada-U.S. border, also influenced his decision.

A justice of the peace, LaRiviere spoke French, English, and seven native dialects, although he could not write his own name. The Aboriginals evidently thought highly of him for one old chieftain who called him White Father (Wakopa) is generally credited with giving the town its name.

One source, however, claims that Wakopa means "broken wheel" and that the name resulted from a battle between the Sioux and Metis during which the

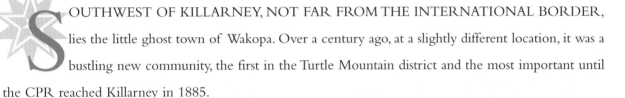

wheel of a Red River cart was broken. Still another interpretation is offered by present-day Sioux and Cree who say it means "flowing water." There is also some difference of opinion as to LaRivere's character. Some settlers complained that he charged outrageous prices until a man named Williams opened a store and provided competition.

In any case, a wave of settlers swept in, more and more land was cultivated and, with hopes of a railway running high, business flourished. In addition to the stores there was a post office, operated initially by LaRiviere's nephew, a creamery (until the cows contracted tuberculosis and had to be destroyed), a sawmill, gristmill, school, roominghouse and several log or sod houses. A number of North-West Mounted Policemen were also present, but lived at the Boundary Commission depot.

The depot apparently lacked kitchen facilities since the officers, like other bachelors in the district, ate at the

Opposite: A photographer takes in the view on the Boundary Commission Trail.

Centre: Finlay Young's home at Wakopa in 1878.

home of Mrs. John Melville. She had arrived at her husband's homestead in 1881 and was the only white woman for miles. Providing food for so many was a problem at times, but she boiled hops for yeast and made bread in a large trough. Rabbits, prairie chickens, and wild fruit helped fill out the menu.

Another problem for residents was the frequent blizzards, which sometimes raged for up to a week. Early homesteader Alex Rankin wrote in his diary about a Hudson's Bay trader who crawled eight km (five miles) from Wood Lake to Wakopa after being out in a blizzard for five days: "The Indians found him and took care of him. They daubed the frozen parts (of his arms and legs) with a knife before thawing so that the congealed blood could ooze out in thawing." According to Rankin, the parts healed perfectly.

In 1885, however, an incident occured that could have had far graver consequences than a blizzard. It was the time of the Riel Rebellion and companies of border wardens were formed in an effort to keep American tribes from joining Riel in Saskatchewan. A large party of Aboriginals passed through Wakopa one day with what they said was the body of their old chief. They were on their way to bury him at the headwaters of Turtle Creek.

Will Moon, an Assiniboine, relayed his suspicions about the band to border wardens Bill Barber and Sam Kellar. Outside Wakopa the Aboriginals were stopped and searched. It was discovered that the so-called coffin was in fact a Gatling gun, which had been smuggled from North Dakota by way of the Missouri Trail.

After that the next major excitement came in the 1920s when Earle Leonard Nelson was captured. He was a vicious killer who preyed on women and had strangled more than twenty. He was finally captured at Wakopa after a ride in a wagon with two unsuspecting children and hanged in Winnipeg in January 1928.

By then Wakopa had joined a growing list of Manitoba communities which had no future. The problem was the railway – or, rather, lack of one. Farmers hauled their wheat to Brandon at first, then to Killarney when the CPR built its line. The new link, however, meant the end of Wakopa's gristmill and when it shut down, so did the sawmill. In 1905 the Canadian Northern Railway ran a line within three km (two miles) of the community but it was not close enough. Businesses once centred at the original Wakopa moved to the railway and a new Wakopa was born.

Among the homes which appeared was a schoolhouse brought in from old Wakopa and converted to a dwelling. It is the only building known to have been moved intact from the old site and by the 1980s was one of only two or three left in Wakopa. The "new" community faded in 1960 when train service was terminated. But as far as one man was concerned it was not quite a ghost town, yet.

Amid the rubble of other men's dreams, cobbler and harness-maker Bill Cullen hoped to build a dream of his own. He and his wife bought most of the townsite in the mid 1960s and granted each of their six children a town lot. When their house burned in April 1979 they put up another, expecting it to be the first of many as their children grew up to raise children of their own. But times change and dreams are put aside. The restoration of Wakopa awaits a new day.

Above: Pupils at Wakopa's first school in the early 1900s.

Below: Aerial view of Wakopa about 1950.

WEST LYNNE

THE AREA IN WHICH WEST LYNNE WOULD EVENTUALLY BE LOCATED was settled as early as 1801 when a fort was built by a Hudson's Bay Company fur trader. Situated at the International Boundary on the banks of the Red River, it later became a stopping place on the Red River cart trail which linked Fort Garry to St. Paul in the United States. Over this trail brigades of creaking Red River carts loaded with furs headed some 1,000 km (600 miles) south-eastward. Since 30 km (20 miles) was a good day's travel for an ox-drawn cart, a return journey took over two months. Nevertheless, from a few carts making the trip in the early 1840s the number grew to over 600 by the late 1850s and peaked a decade later when some 2,500 were engaged.

In those days the exact location of the boundary separating Canada and the United States was not entirely clear – a matter which often caused confusion. Once, a young missionary who had been travelling through the United States, stayed at the fort and was so overcome with joy at being back in Canada, that he sang a stirring rendition of God Save the Queen. His show of patriotism proved premature. Shortly after, the International Boundary Commission determined that the fort was actually in American territory.

The same mistake was made by other visitors – notably a band of Fenian raiders in 1871. The Fenians were members of an organization founded in New York in the 1850s to seek independence for Ireland. They were avowed English haters. An official report by their leader, General John O'Neil, stated in part: "As to the propriety of invading Canada, I have always had but one opinion: Canada is a province of Great Britain; the British flag floats over it and English soldiers protect it, and, I think, wherever the English flag and English soldiers are found, Irishmen have a right to attack."

The attack on West Lynne is mentioned by one of the residents, Frank Bouvette, in his memoirs: "I was ten years old when a band of Fenians, led by J.B. O'Donahue, captured the Hudson's Bay Company's store at West Lynne…At the time there were four villages in the vicinity, known locally as the 'four corners'."

(The four villages were West Lynne and Emerson on either side of the Red River in Canada, and Pembina and St. Vincent on either side of the Red River in the United States. Between Pembina and West Lynne there

Opposite: In the late 1850s some 2,500 Red River carts were used in freighting on the cart trail which passed through West Lynne.

was a garrison of six companies of United States foot soldiers commanded by a Captain Wheaton.)

"We were then living at Pembina. That morning my mother and I and a younger brother drove to West Lynne to get some things from the store. As soon as we drove up one of O'Donahue's men tied our horses up and made us prisoners. A short time after, Mrs. Wheaton, the Captain's wife, was driven up by one of the soldiers from the fort, and they were treated in a similar manner. Soon there were about twenty-seven of us all prisoners, and all herded together in a large log storehouse which happened to be empty at the time. It had a cellar, and we soon found that I was small enough to crawl through an opening in the wall...They gave me very minute instructions as to what I should do."

Young Bouvette made his escape and, with a note to Captain Wheaton pinned inside his coat, made his way back to the fort. "Instantly the 'long roll' was sounded and in a very short time two companies of soldiers were on the march with two cannons, while I trailed along behind to see what would happen," he recalled.

"It would appear that when Captain Wheaton advanced on the store O'Donahue was taken entirely by surprise. When they arrived the soldiers deployed in single file so as to surround the store, but before the cordon was complete a lot of Fenians, including O'Donahue, made a break for liberty. Some of them swam (the) Red River in their eagerness to escape. O'Donahue was later captured by two Canadians about five miles north of West Lynne and handed over to Captain Wheaton.

"My recollection of the matter is that about forty prisoners were taken...Later on from time to time I saw these men working around the fort, shovelling snow, etc...None of them were punished for taking part in the raid."

According to Bouvette: "Had he (O'Donahue) succeeded in establishing himself at West Lynne, he might have caused the Canadian Government a great deal of trouble and annoyance. West Lynne might have become the rallying point for all the disaffected in the country, and for other Fenians in the United States. But he blundered when he made Mrs. Wheaton and the United States soldiers prisoners. Had it not been for that strate-

Below: The sternwheel steamer *Assiniboine* on the main street in Emerson during the 1897 Red River flood.

Above: Unloading baggage car.

gic error, it is unlikely Captain Wheaton would have led an armed force into British territory for the purpose of turning a handful of Fenians out of a Hudson's Bay store."

While the Hudson's Bay Company had been the first to capitalize on the region's fur resource, it was the Americans who realized the agricultural potential of the fertile Red River Valley. To help solve the transportation problem, in 1859 they launched the *North Star*, a sternwheel steamer. Others followed, including the *Northwest* and the *International*, the latter capable of making the 885 km (550 mile) trip from Fargo-Moorhead to Winnipeg in about six days.

Since the only route to eastern Canada from Fort Garry was that used by the voyageurs and their birch bark canoes, these sternwheelers were the lifeline for pioneer residents. Dan Lewis, an Emerson resident, said: "Many of the Mennonites west of town came down the river from Fargo on the *Cheyenne*. They say there were seven babies born between Fargo and West Lynne. A very prolific people!"

This boat is mentioned in an 1881 report by the *Nelsonville Manitoba Mountaineer:* "The steamer *Cheyenne* continues to make her trips as regular as the sun rises and sets, every Sunday and Thursday, the favourite boat puts in her appearance at the levee. She is doing a good local business, and we are informed that West Lynne is considered the best town on the river for steamboat trade."

West Lynne had now developed into a refuelling point for the steamers. After the location of the boundary had been determined, it also acquired a customs building which served as a telegraph, express and post office.

While West Lynne's fortunes were rising, two American entrepreneurs sought to save the languishing sister village of Emerson from oblivion. Their motive, however, wasn't entirely unselfish since Emerson was in the path of two proposed rail lines – the Canadian Pacific's Pembina branch and the St. Paul and Pacific from the United States. The entrepreneurs visualized the location as money in the bank.

While the American line did arrive in 1879 and Emerson began to grow, its businessmen worried because West Lynne, which had received official status as a townsite that same year, was growing even faster. There was no bridge across the river and the ferry was almost useless for transporting goods because of the river's steep banks. West Lynne, therefore, got all the trade from the west – including that of the large new Mennonite population.

Elizabeth Bergen, daughter of a Mennonite pioneer, recalled: "I remember my dad saying that they'd go to West Lynne for the mail, travelling along the 'post road'. It ran east and west parallel to the U.S. boundary and got its name from the poles the Mennonites put in so they could see to find their way; in winter because of the snow drifts and in summer because of the tall buffalo grass. It was the main artery. It's still there off Highway 13 a mile north of Gretna, but the posts are all gone now."

Above: The 100-year-old Canadian customs house above was mistakenly built in North Dakota. When the error was discovered, it was quickly moved to West Lynne. It was restored and used as a museum until being vandalized.

West Lynne continued to prosper, its business places including four general stores, six hotels, a brewery where a six-quart pail of beer was 15 cents (cash and carry), a pop factory, five implement agencies, cheese factory, two churches, a school and even a newspaper, *The West Lynne and Southern Manitoba Times.*

West Lynne seemed to be winning the race for survival and the Emersonians across the river were jealous. An item in the *Manitoba Mountaineer* illustrates the depth of the resentment: "The latest way the *International* (Emerson's newspaper) endeavours to ignore West Lynne is by saying 'the half-mile track west of town'. Everyone knows as a matter of fact that the race track is in West Lynne and not in Emerson…If the people of Emerson really wish to cultivate a good spirit with the people of West Lynne they should set, not an example of selfishness and untruthfulness, but rather one of fair play and magnanimity…"

The rivalry intensified when, in early 1881, West Lynne businessmen announced that, to counter Emerson's new Emerson and Turtle Mountain Railway Company, they were planning a railway of their own. It was to be called The West Lynne, Rhineland and Rock Lake Railway and would run southwest through the fertile Mennonite Reserve. One problem was that the name was almost as long as the proposed trackage. Nevertheless, the *Manitoba Mountaineer* noted: "We have heard of several good trades and sales of West Lynne real estate lately. Lots have decidedly an upward tendency since the railway news."

The future looked bright for both towns. Then, in a new spirit of generosity and co-operation with Emerson, West Lynne agreed to provide $60,000 for construction of a bridge provided that the station and freight yards were built inside the town limits of West Lynne.

To solidify and enhance the new relationship, officials from both towns agreed to incorporate West Lynne and Emerson. As a consequence, in 1883 the two adopted the impressive name, City of Emerson. Unfortunately, the visions of prosperity soon shattered and the community found not a pot of gold at the end of their optimism but a monumental debt.

Dreamers on both sides of the river had neglected to take into account the CPR's monopoly agreement with the federal government. It stated that no charters would be issued for another railway to build south of its transcontinental line. The promoters of the Emerson and Turtle Mountain Railway Company, however, were certain that the provincial government would make some provisions for their project. Having convinced themselves, they formed a mortgage and holding company to raise the capital.

West Lynne historian Dan Lewis explained the consequence: "They were granted a charter from the provincial government but the federal government overrode it and they (the Emerson company) had already borrowed thousands of dollars to build the bridge and had started building the railway. They put in tracks as far as Horndean – about 20 or 25 miles – but they had to tear it all up and quit because the monopoly clause said that no one would build south of the CPR."

They managed to keep the bridge, but not without a struggle. "They couldn't pay the contractor," said Lewis. "It was one of those railway bridges that could swing open in the centre and let the river traffic through. So the contractor said, 'If you can't pay me, you're not going to use it.' He swung the bridge across and camped up on the centre pier with the big turnkey – the tool he used to turn the bridge. The citizens wanted to use the bridge in the worst way, so, in the night some of them got in a boat and drifted down to the pier. Then they climbed up and overpowered the contractor but in the scuffle he threw the key into the river. Anyway, when they finally got him on shore, they made some kind of deal with him and then they fished the key out of the river and put the bridge back into operation."

Not all problems were resolved so amicably. The railway and bridge debts combined with land deals and shady politics bankrupted the newly formed City of Emerson. In addition, an investigation revealed that town affairs had been mismanaged to an appalling degree. As a result, citizens and aldermen disagreed to the point of a fist fight and at least two of the town's leading citizens fled in humiliation and fear for their lives.

Although Emerson had achieved a phenomenal growth of over 3,000 people during the early 1880s, by 1886 there were only about 600 left. In a classic understatement, Lewis noted, "They owed a lot of money."

The same year the Municipal Act divided the City of Emerson back into the two towns of Emerson and West Lynne. Local politics continued to be conducted in such a dubious manner that special policemen were engaged to supervise voting procedures. Finally, in 1888,

Above: George Pocock's house is the only original building still standing in West Lynne.

when the political and financial situations began to stabilize with help from the provincial government, the two towns were once again united. This time, not as the grandiose City of Emerson but as the more modest Town of Emerson.

Not only had the railway bubble burst, but by then the steamboat transportation system on the Red River ceased to function. Fighting between the two rival companies (a ship was rammed and sunk during the hostilities) resulted in one company holding a monopoly. The disillusioned public stopped supporting it. The promised CPR branch line missed Emerson by 35 km (22 miles) and all that was left was local trade.

Gradually, most of what had been West Lynne moved across the river to Emerson. The only original West Lynne building standing is George Pocock's house – an imposing structure that Pocock built to appease his wife who wouldn't move to Canada until she had a duplicate of her home in England.

...AN INVESTIGATION REVEALED THAT TOWN AFFAIRS HAD BEEN MISMANAGED TO AN APPALLING DEGREE.

WHITEWATER

H ONESTY IN ADVERTISING WAS NOT A RECOGNIZED CONCEPT in the early days. Along with snake oil salesmen, real estate brokers were not above manipulating the truth or ignoring it altogether. In an early attempt to lure prospective settlers to the west, large colourful posters showed steamboats plying the raging waters of Whitewater Lake. This lake, in fact, was a shallow body of water about fifteen miles long and six miles wide according to an early settler's report. In addition, it sometimes disappeared completely during dry years.

THE FIRST STATION AGENT IN WHITEWATER, AN AMERICAN NAMED SIMPSON, APPARENTLY WAS A SURVIVOR OF CUSTER'S MASSACRE.

However, if the lake wasn't a sufficient draw in and of itself, the surrounding area of lush hay lands was. According to information given in the local history book, *Beckoning Hills Revisited*, George Morton, a cheese maker from Kingston, Ontario, saw the potential for large-scale dairy farming which he hoped would support a thriving cheese industry. To this end, in 1878, he persuaded a group of businessmen to invest in The Morton Dairy Farm Company and acquired permission from the Dominion Government to purchase a tract of government land.

Three years later his plans were in place with settlers geared up to supply the milk needed for cheese production. Morton built a sawmill and gristmill for dairymen's needs and a town site was laid out at Whitewater Lake to provide a community and business centre. Unfortunately, the grandiose scheme failed. Inappropriate over-wintering of cattle in the harsh prairie climate resulted in massive losses and, in any case, no railway

appeared in time to transport the hoped-for cheese to markets.

During these years, settlers were moving into the area from Great Britain and Ontario. They endured the arduous journey to Emerson by rail and then west by ox cart, covered wagons and sleighs. Although another town site, Wabeesh, was established to serve their needs, it was abandoned in 1887 because the Southwestern Colonization Railway had gone two miles north to Whitewater the year before.

The first station agent in Whitewater, an American named Simpson, apparently was a survivor of Custer's massacre. His escape across the border from North Dakota to Manitoba was accomplished because his job as signalman saw him out in the hills during the Sioux attack. Another version of the story, though partially in agreement with the above, states that Simpson, who was a telegraph operator, was indeed on watch in the hills. It differs, though, in what transpired later. The allegation is

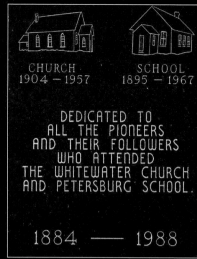

CHURCH
1904 — 1957

SCHOOL
1895 — 1967

DEDICATED TO
ALL THE PIONEERS
AND THEIR FOLLOWERS
WHO ATTENDED
THE WHITEWATER CHURCH
AND PETERSBURG SCHOOL.

1884 ——— 1988

Left: A quiet place to reminisce.

A 1914 FIRE THAT DESTROYED THE
BLACKSMITH SHOP ALSO BURNED
THE STORE, BUT A NEW ONE WAS BUILT
TO REPLACE IT.

that Simpson saw the Sioux approach, flashed a warning signal to the troops and then made fast tracks to safety in Canada where he could not be charged with desertion.

Meanwhile, George Morton, recognizing the advantage of having a new site built on the rail line, used the lumber from his existing sawmill to build an elevator, store and boarding house. Soon, four more elevators were built as well as a lumber yard. By the turn of the century, Whitewater boasted a butcher shop, harness-making shop, skating rink, livery stable, blacksmith, a local carpenter and a draftsman as well as a machinery agency. Also, the multi-talented Mr. Peters, who managed Mr. Morton's store and post office, acted as resident doctor, veterinarian, dentist, magistrate and livery man.

A 1914 fire that destroyed the blacksmith shop also burned the store, but a new one was built to replace it. Then, as Whitewater welcomed a number of new settlers, another store was opened in a house. This was later replaced with another in a different location. Fuel distribution centres appeared and a blacksmith shop opened for business again, too.

A brick yard played a large part in the town's economy. Built in the late 1880s, and using clay from Whitewater Lake, it employed over thirty men and when it was sold and relocated to Deloraine in 1894, its loss was keenly felt by the community. The enterprise had supplied bricks for many of the local buildings as well as the Petersburg School.

In the beginning, church services were held in homes. In 1894, however, when the school building was erected, services were held there with a Presbyterian minister from Ninga presiding. In 1904, the congregation laid the cornerstone for a handsome stone church which served the area for forty-three years before being demolished.

Petersburg School was also well used as a community centre for meetings, dances and various social events. In 1957, a new school was built giving hope to the community that Whitewater would not die as so many other towns were doing. It lasted ten years – until all the rural schools were consolidated.

The Canadian Pacific Railway built a stock yard with loading ramps, dug a reservoir and erected a water storage tank. They had provided daily freight, mail and passenger service to Whitewater, but the latter two were discontinued in the early 1930s.

Oil was discovered in the area in 1953, and although there are still some wells in production, not enough revenue was produced to prop up a community in serious decline.

Consolidation of rural schools and the loss of rail passenger, mail and freight service played a part. Given the trend to larger farms with smaller populations who had easy transportation to larger towns with better shopping facilities, the end was predictable. All that remains of the village is the building that housed a store until 1963. Later used as a residence, it now serves as a hunting lodge.

YORK FACTORY

ALTHOUGH YORK FACTORY ON THE SHORE OF HUDSON BAY cannot be called a ghost town since it never was a town, its ruins are nevertheless a direct link to Manitoba's first permanent settlement. This settlement was on the Red River near modern-day Winnipeg and dates back to 1811. But well before then York Factory had another distinction – supply point for a region of some 3.9 million square km (1.5 million square miles), over one-third of the land that became Canada.

York Factory was built in 1682 as a Hudson's Bay Company fur-trading post where the Hayes and Nelson Rivers flow into Hudson Bay. Although it was of great strategic importance, in 1714 HBC Governor James Knight wasn't impressed with it. His unflattering observation was that it was "…nothing but a confused heap of old rotten houses without form or strength…My own place I have to live in this winter is not half so good as our cowhouse was in the Bottom of the Bay."

The British and French did not agree with Knight's assessment. To them possession of it was vital in their bitter rivalry to control the fur trade and, in the early years, they took turns occupying York Factory. For this reason it underwent several name changes. Its first name dates to 1670 when Pierre Radisson and Charles Bayly were sent by the Governor and Company of Adventurers Trading into Hudson Bay to establish a settlement. Thus appeared the first of a series of forts built by the Hudson's Bay Company. Eventually they would extend westward over 3,200 km (2,000 miles) to the Pacific Ocean, with the one built on the north shore of the Hayes River called Fort Hayes.

Later, to honour the Duke of York, the name was changed to York Fort. But when the French captured the fort in 1694, they renamed it Bourbon. Except for a brief period in 1696 when it was recaptured by the English, the name remained until the Treaty of Utrecht in 1713 gave the Hudson's Bay Company complete authority over the Hudson Bay region.

Over the years floods and fires resulted in York Fort being moved several times but owing to the meticulous preservation of records by the Hudson's Bay Company, this phase of its history is well documented. Descriptions of life at the fort are also contained in journals and letters of company employees, their families, explorers and other travellers.

A description in 1686 was left by a Frenchman, Nicolas Jeremie: "The fort had four bastions, forming a square of thirty feet, in which was a large warehouse of two stories. The trading store was in one of these bas-

Opposite: York Factory from the air, circa 1926.

tions, another served as a supply store, and the other two were used as guard houses to hold the garrison.

"The whole was built of wood. In line with the first palisade were two other bastions, in one of which officers lodged, the other serving as a kitchen and forge for the garrison. Between these two bastions was a kind of half-moon space in which were eight cannon, throwing an eight-pound ball, which commanded the river side. Below this half-moon space was a platform, at the level of the water, which held six pieces of heavy cannon. No cannon was mounted on the side of the wood; all the cannon and swivel guns were on the bastions. There were altogether in the fort, which had only two palisades of upright logs, thirty-two cannon and fourteen swivel guns. There were fifty-three men in the fort."

In 1714, when Knight was sent to accept the French surrender, the fort was named York Factory. (The word "factory" was used to describe the residence of an agent, or factor.) Its dilapidated condition was beyond repair so Knight decided to build the new fort just downstream. Because construction couldn't begin until the following spring. Knight and his men had to spend an uncomfortable winter in the decaying structure. "…the best place to lye our Goods was out of Doors for there it was dry over head wn. Done raineing," Knight wrote, "but in the houses wee had the Drapping of them for Some hours after."

The next year they were able to move into their new quarters: "…the best Lodging as ever man had in this Country." Then in 1716, after a second storey was added for storing dry goods and skins, Knight described it as: "…36 foot square wth. A Crane to hoist goods up by." A palisade was built and the Company continued to add to the fort. In 1718 Henry Kelsey, who had replaced Knight, mentioned the addition of guns, a cookroom, powder room, smithy and trading room.

In spite of the fact that marshy ground offered a poor foundation, buildings continued to be of logs. In 1745 Joseph Robson, a stone mason, noted: "York Fort stands above high-water mark, about eight yards from Hayes's River, and four miles from the sea. It is built with logs of white fir eight or nine inches square, which are laid one upon the other. In the summer the water beats between the logs, keeping the timber continually damp; and in the winter the white frost gets through, which being thawed by the heat of the stoves, has the same effect: so that with the water above and the damp below, the timber both of the foundation and super-structure rots so fast, that in twenty-five or thirty years the whole fort must be rebuilt with fresh timber, which with the great quantity used for firing will occasion a scarcity there in a few years."

Robson also mentioned that the four bastions were not fit for cannon and needed a drainage ditch. In 1763 permission was given to bring stone from Churchill to rebuild the fort but the project was never completed. Staff quarters, however, were enlarged in the late 1770s when extra men were posted to York to assist with some of the Company's inland forts. But in 1782 the French

"…THE BEST PLACE TO LYE OUR GOODS WAS OUT OF DOORS FOR THERE IT WAS DRY OVER HEAD WN. DONE RAINEING…"

Below: York Factory in the early 1900s.

again captured the fort and this time burned it. In the next year the British drove the French out but because of the destruction had to have a prefabricated building sent from England to house the trade goods.

When the plans for a new fort arrived, Joseph Colen, Officer in Charge, did not approve them. He prepared to proceed with his own design which he said "…would be equally lasting and strong, as the flankers…which are to be built with Logs for warmth – between each Curtain and flanker – a stone or Brick wall will be built to prevent fire communicating in case of accident."

It was not fire, however, that would prove a problem but flood. The following spring Hayes River rose 9.7 metres (32 feet) and a new location was chosen about 1.6 km farther up the river on higher ground. The rebuilding project progressed with dismal slowness. A Company employee complained in 1798 that "the whole Building is a mere Shell and more calculated for Show than anything else…The Cellars within the Factory must be pumped every two or three days."

The fort was built in the form of an octagon, inside a square of palisades 5.4 metres (18 feet) high, but there were no bastions. Of it one visitor wrote: "Between the Stockades and Octagon are a few scattered houses for the men employed at the Fort. The Governor's abode, Officers rooms, and the Warehouses are all under one roof, and these buildings are of wood, and the rooms warmed by the means of stoves, so dangerously constructed by the pipes running

Above: The sketch above shows York Factory in 1853. It began as a log trading post nearly 200 years before.

through the roof, that it is astonishing to me no accident has happened by fire."

In 1811 the first people not associated with the fur trade arrived on the ship *Edward and Ann*. They were a contingent of colonists under the leadership of Miles Macdonnell, bound for Lord Selkirk's Red River settlement near today's Winnipeg. Two days later another ship, the *Eddystone*, enroute to Churchill, had to put in at York Factory because of the lateness of the season. This influx of unexpected visitors severely strained the fort's facilities, as well as relations between the newcomers and the Company's employees.

A camp to accommodate some of the men was established some distance away in an area where it was thought game would be plentiful. However, it was spring before any deer were shot and Macdonnell made himself unpopular by asking for more and better rations than those at the fort were receiving. He compounded his bad judgement by arbitrarily dividing the camp, giving himself twenty-one more men than Hillier who commanded the Hudson's Bay servants. Nor did his popularity increase when he tried to lure away Company employees for his own settlement at Red River.

In that outpost Macdonnell's presence was as disruptive as a hawk in a chicken coop – and about as welcome. For this reason York Factory residents bade him and his little group of settlers a hearty farewell in July 1812, nine months after their arrival. Fortunately, circumstances surrounding subsequent accommodation of settlers was more favourable, largely because earlier arrival of ships allowed time for the travellers to continue with only brief stopovers at the fort.

Besides settlers, York Factory hosted a variety of interesting visitors during the 19th century. Among them were missionaries, botanists, soldiers, geologists and explorers. One of the most famous arrived in 1819 after a fourteen-week journey from England. He was Captain John Franklin who earned great respect from residents by seeking their advice on Arctic travel, including the best routes to the Arctic Ocean.

Governor Williams was happy to assist and the company men presented Franklin with a large riverboat to use in his exploration and mapping. Twenty-eight years later, Franklin and his entire crew of 129 men disappeared during an expedition to locate the North-west Passage.

Over the years York Factory grew slowly; new buildings included stores, a powder magazine and winter dwelling houses. By 1830 when Governor Simpson brought his bride she wrote: "In the shops one can buy groceries, haberdashery, ironmongery, cutlery, medicines,

Above: Earlier arrival of ships allowed time for travellers to continue inland with only a brief stopover at the Fort.

OVER THE YEARS
YORK FACTORY
GREW SLOWLY;
NEW BUILDINGS
INCLUDED STORES,
A POWDER MAGA-
ZINE AND WINTER
DWELLING HOUSES.

and even perfumery at prices lower than the same articles could be had at, in any retail shop in London."

During the next decade work began on a great depot building. In 1840 Mrs. Hargrave, the wife of a company employee, described the Factory in glowing terms in a letter to her mother: "I was much surprised at the 'great swell' the Factory is. It looks beautiful. The houses are painted pale yellow. The windows and some particular parts white. Some have green gauze mosquito curtains outside and the effect is very good."

By the mid 1850s York Factory reached its peak. Afterwards, because of rival American routes, the Hudson's Bay Company was obliged to find other trade routes to serve their array of inland posts. As a result 1873 was the fort's last season of any importance. It was gradually superseded by Fort Garry, another HBC fort established at the junction of the Red and Assiniboine Rivers in the early 1800s.

No longer did the "Kichewaskahikan" (the Aboriginal name for the great depot) echo with shouts of busy men bringing in the cargoes of wine, tobacco, food and trade goods or attending the flotillas of Aboriginal canoes packed with furs for barter. York Factory was left to handle only the coastal trade, just as it had done in the beginning. It did, however, continue to provide this service until 1957 when the old fort was closed, bringing to an end 275 years of continuous service – a record in a country as young as Canada.

York Factory is now a National Historic Site and has been under the jurisdiction of Parks Canada since 1969. In 1991, excavations began and major archeological work is being done on the old Hudson's Bay Company Depot which is the largest and oldest wooden building standing on permafrost in Canada. The long-term plan includes stabilization and repairs and the rescue of any artifacts that might be damaged in the process.

The site is staffed by Parks Canada from June 1st to mid September, but access is by air or water only.

PHOTO CREDITS

All photographs in this book are courtesy
of the Provincial Archives of Manitoba,
except as follows:

The Authors: pages 4, 6, 8, 11, 18, 19, 21, 31, 33, 34, 39,
56, 61, 62, 66, 70, 71, 72, 75, 76, 77, 83, 86, 88, 89, 92, 93,
94, 95, 96, 99, 101, 106, 112, 113, 114, 115, 117, 131, 132.

Charlie Baldock: 9, 125, 126
Bernice Blixhaven: 10, 12, 124,
Canadian Pacific Railway: 91, 110
Daly House, Brandon: 29
Charles L. D'Aoust: 23, 43, 46, 108
Tom Hall: 74
W. E. Mason: 44, 45, 46
Ste-Elizabeth Historical Committee: 116, 117, 118, 119
Don Sanderson: 80, 81, 87, 88, 133, 134
Western Canada Pictorial Index: 65

Cindy Williams: cover photo of hay barn and
milk barn at Mountain Road.

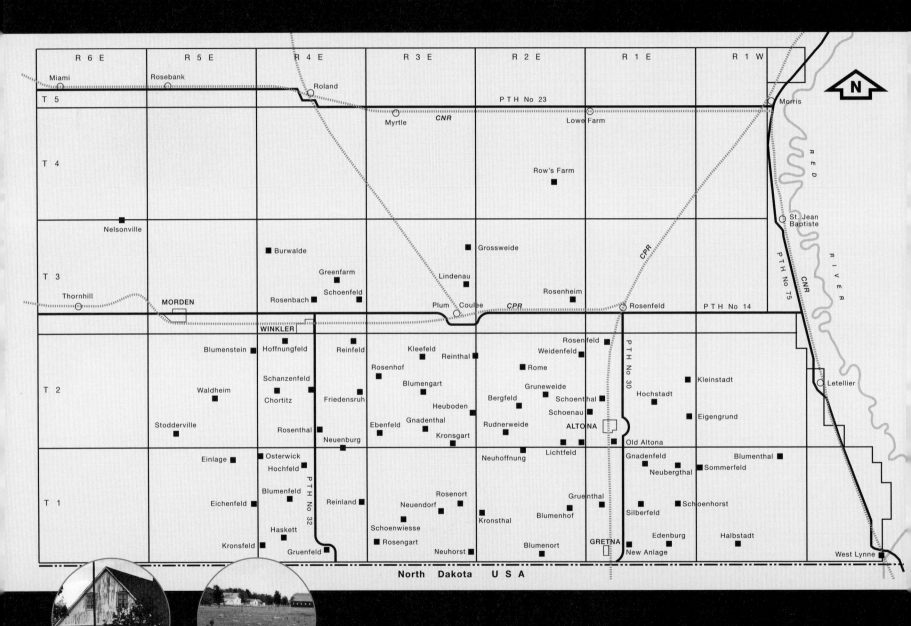

| R 6 E | R 5 E | R 4 E | R 3 E | R 2 E | R 1 E | R 1 W |

Miami   Rosebank
                          Roland
T 5   P T H No 23   Morris

                                    Myrtle   CNR   Lowe Farm
T 4
                                                        Row's Farm

                                                                                                    St. Jean Baptiste
Nelsonville

                            Burwalde   Grossweide
T 3   Greenfarm
                                          Lindenau   Rosenheim   CPR
         Thornhill   Schoenfeld
                            Rosenbach   Plum Coulee   CPR   Rosenfeld   P T H No 14
         MORDEN

         WINKLER
                                                              Rosenfeld
         Blumenstein   Hoffnungfeld   Reinfeld   Kleefeld   Weidenfeld
                                          Rosenhof   Reinthal   Rome
                      Schanzenfeld   Blumengart   Gruneweide
T 2   Waldheim   Friedensruh   Bergfeld   Schoenthal   Kleinstadt
                      Chortitz   Heuboden   Schoenau   Hochstadt
         Stodderville   Rosenthal   Ebenfeld   Gnadenthal   Rudnerweide   ALTONA   Eigengrund
                            Neuenburg   Kronsgart   Old Altona
                                                              Lichtfeld
                      Osterwick   Neuhoffnung   Gnadenfeld   Blumenthal
         Einlage   Hochfeld   Neubergthal   Sommerfeld
                      Blumenfeld   Gruenthal
T 1   Reinland   Rosenort   Blumenhof   Silberfeld   Schoenhorst
         Eichenfeld   Neuendorf   Kronsthal
                      Haskett   Schoenwiesse   Blumenort   GRETNA   Edenburg   Halbstadt
         Kronsfeld   Gruenfeld   Rosengart   Neuhorst   New Anlage   West Lynne

         North Dakota U S A

INDEX

NOTES

Publications of particular help to the authors in the revision and expansion of *Ghost Towns of Manitoba* are as follows: *Along the Hills to the Valley, Huns Valley Polonia District 1885-1985* by William R. Smith; *Rosedale Remembers 1884-1984*, published by the *Rural Municipality of Rosedale; Reapers of the Valley 1882-1982*, by Claire DeSharnais, published by the Montcalm History Group; *Of Days Gone By, a history of the Ste. Elizabeth District*, published 1970 by the Mennonite Centennial Reunion Committee; *Manitoba: A History*, by W. L. Morton, University of Toronto Press 1976; the *Canadian Historical Review, Volume 21*, 1940; *Cuthbert Grant of Grantown* by Margaret Arnett MacLeod, McClelland and Stewart 1963; *Songs of Old Manitoba* by Margaret Arnett Macleod, published by Ryerson Press; *Cuthbert Grant and the Metis* by D. Bruce Sealey, Book Society of Canada Limited; *The Red River Settlement* by Keith Wilson, Grolier Limited; *A History, Manitoba 125*, volume 1, published by Great Plains. *Speaking of Spearhill* compiled by L.Jean Jardine; *The Holland History Book* (1967); *Beckoning Hills Revisited* (1981); *From the Past to the Present* (1898-1967); *A History of Rossburn and District*; *Echoes* (Oakburn Centennial History (1879-1970).